Eighth Workshop on Building and Using Comparable Corpora 2015

Co-located with ACL-IJCNLP 2015

Beijing, China
30 July 2015

ISBN: 978-1-5108-0946-8

Printed from e-media with permission by:

Curran Associates, Inc.
57 Morehouse Lane
Red Hook, NY 12571

Some format issues inherent in the e-media version may also appear in this print version.

Printed by Curran Associates, Inc. (2015)

For permission requests, please contact the Association for Computational Linguistics at the address below.

Association for Computational Linguistics
209 N. Eighth Street
Stroudsburg, Pennsylvania 18360

Phone: 1-570-476-8006
Fax: 1-570-476-0860

acl@aclweb.org

Additional copies of this publication are available from:

Curran Associates, Inc.
57 Morehouse Lane
Red Hook, NY 12571 USA
Phone: 845-758-0400
Fax: 845-758-2634
Email: curran@proceedings.com
Web: www.proceedings.com

ACL-IJCNLP 2015

Eighth Workshop on
Building and Using Comparable Corpora

Proceedings of the Workshop

July 30, 2015
Beijing, China

Production and Manufacturing by
Taberg Media Group AB
Box 94, 562 02 Taberg
Sweden

Introduction to BUCC 2015

Comparable corpora are collections of documents that are comparable in content and form in various degrees and dimensions. This definition includes many types of parallel and non-parallel multilingual corpora, but also sets of monolingual corpora that are used for comparative purposes. Research on comparable corpora is active but used to be scattered among many workshops and conferences. The workshop series on "Building and Using Comparable Corpora" (BUCC) aims at promoting progress in this exciting emerging field by bundling its research, thereby making it more visible and giving it a better platform.

Research on comparable corpora spans a number of topics from machine translation to contrastive linguistics. Distributional analysis, a topic which has seen renewed interest in recent years, has formed the core of a large part of the methods used to identify translations in comparable corpora. As a matter of fact, the standard techniques of word alignment in comparable corpora can be seen as methods for cross-language distributional semantics.

Following the seven previous editions of the workshop which took place at LREC 2008 (Marrakech), ACL-IJCNLP 2009 (Singapore), LREC 2010 (Malta), ACL-HLT 2011 (Portland), LREC 2012 (Istanbul), ACL 2013 (Sofia), LREC 2014 (Reykjavik), the workshop this year is co-located with ACL-IJCNLP 2015 in Beijing, China.

This year's workshop also hosts a companion shared task which is the first evaluation exercise on the identification of comparable texts: given a large multilingual collection of texts derived from Wikipedia, detecting the most similar texts across languages. Evaluation is performed using a gold standard based on actual inter-language links. Three teams submitted eleven runs to link text in three languages to comparable English texts. A special section in this proceedings volume reports on this shared task.

Finally, we would like to thank all people who in one way or another helped in making this workshop once again a success. Our special thanks go to Benjamin K. Tsou for accepting to give the invited presentation, to the members of the program committee who did an excellent job in reviewing the submitted papers, and to the ACL-IJCNLP 2015 workshop chairs and organizers. We also thank LIMSI-CNRS for financial support to our invited speaker. Last but not least we would like to thank our authors and the participants of the workshop.

Pierre Zweigenbaum, Serge Sharoff, Reinhard Rapp

Organizers

Pierre Zweigenbaum LIMSI, CNRS, Orsay (France), Chair
Serge Sharoff University of Leeds (UK), Shared Task Chair
Reinhard Rapp University of Mainz (Germany)

Programme Committee

Ahmet Aker, University of Sheffield (UK)
Srinivas Bangalore (AT&T Labs, US)
Caroline Barrière (CRIM, Montréal, Canada)
Hervé Déjean (Xerox Research Centre Europe, Grenoble, France)
Kurt Eberle (Lingenio, Heidelberg, Germany)
Andreas Eisele (European Commission, Luxembourg)
Éric Gaussier (Université Joseph Fourier, Grenoble, France)
Gregory Grefenstette (INRIA, Saclay, France)
Silvia Hansen-Schirra (University of Mainz, Germany)
Hitoshi Isahara (Toyohashi University of Technology)
Kyo Kageura (University of Tokyo, Japan)
Adam Kilgarriff (Lexical Computing Ltd, UK)
Natalie Kübler (Université Paris Diderot, France)
Philippe Langlais (Université de Montréal, Canada)
Michael Mohler (Language Computer Corp., US)
Emmanuel Morin (Université de Nantes, France)
Dragos Stefan Munteanu (Language Weaver, Inc., US)
Lene Offersgaard (University of Copenhagen, Denmark)
Ted Pedersen (University of Minnesota, Duluth, US)
Reinhard Rapp (Université Aix-Marseille, France)
Sujith Ravi (Google, US)
Serge Sharoff (University of Leeds, UK)
Michel Simard (National Research Council Canada)
Tim Van de Cruys (IRIT-CNRS, Toulouse, France)
Stephan Vogel, QCRI (Qatar)
Guillaume Wisniewski (Université Paris Sud & LIMSI-CNRS, Orsay, France)
Pierre Zweigenbaum (LIMSI-CNRS, Orsay, France)

Invited Speaker

Benjamin K. Tsou (City University of Hong Kong)

Table of Contents

Workshop Program

Thursday, July 30, 2015

Session 1: 09:00–10:30 Opening Session

09:00–09:05 *Introduction to the BUCC Workshop*
Pierre Zweigenbaum, Serge Sharoff, Reinhard Rapp

09:05–10:05 **Invited presentation:** *Augmented Comparative Corpora and Monitoring Corpus in Chinese: LIVAC and Sketch Search Engine Compared*
Benjamin K. Tsou

10:05–10:30 *A Factory of Comparable Corpora from Wikipedia*
Alberto Barrón-Cedeño, Cristina España-Bonet, Josu Boldoba and Lluís Màrquez

Session 2: 11:00–12:30

11:00–11:25 *Knowledge-lean projection of coreference chains across languages*
Yulia Grishina and Manfred Stede

11:25–11:50 *Projective methods for mining missing translations in DBpedia*
Laurent Jakubina and Philippe Langlais

11:50–12:05 *Attempting to Bypass Alignment from Comparable Corpora via Pivot Language*
Alexis Linard, Béatrice Daille and Emmanuel Morin

12:05–12:20 *Application of a Corpus to Identify Gaps between English Learners and Native Speakers*
Katsunori Kotani and Takehiko Yoshimi

Thursday, July 30, 2015 (continued)

Session 3: 14:00–15:30 Alignment

14:00–14:25 *A Generative Model for Extracting Parallel Fragments from Comparable Documents*
Somayeh Bakhshaei, Shahram Khadivi and Reza Safabakhsh

14:25–14:50 *Evaluating Features for Identifying Japanese-Chinese Bilingual Synonymous Technical Terms from Patent Families*
Zi Long, Takehito Utsuro, Tomoharu Mitsuhashi and Mikio Yamamoto

14:50–15:05 *Extracting Bilingual Lexica from Comparable Corpora Using Self-Organizing Maps*
Hyeong-Won Seo, Minah Cheon and Jae-Hoon Kim

15:05–15:20 *Obtaining SMT dictionaries for related languages*
Miguel Rios and Serge Sharoff

Session 4: 16:00–17:00 Shared Task

16:00–16:15 *BUCC Shared Task: Cross-Language Document Similarity*
Serge Sharoff, Pierre Zweigenbaum and Reinhard Rapp

16:15–16:30 *AUT Document Alignment Framework for BUCC Workshop Shared Task*
Atefeh Zafarian, Amir Pouya Agha Sadeghi, Fatemeh Azadi, Sonia Ghiasifard, Zeinab Ali Panahloo, Somayeh Bakhshaei and Seyyed Mohammad Mohammadzadeh Ziabary

16:30–16:45 *LINA: Identifying Comparable Documents from Wikipedia*
Emmanuel Morin, Amir Hazem, Florian Boudin and Elizaveta Loginova-Clouet

16:45–17:00 *Shared Task: General Discussion*

Closing: 17:00

Augmented Comparative Corpora and Monitoring Corpus in Chinese: LIVAC and Sketch Search Engine Compared

Benjamin K. Tsou
City University of Hong Kong,
The Chinese University of Hong Kong,
Hong Kong University of Science and Technology

The increasing availability of numerous corpora has significantly contributed to the understanding of words in terms of their underlying semantic structures and lexical networks (e.g. COBUILD, WordNet etc.). Through data mining and information retrieval, research in this area has vastly expanded our appreciation that what constitutes lexical knowledge goes beyond synonymy, hyponymy, metonymy, meronymy, grammatical and other collocations. Furthermore, they are fundamental to a universalistic conceptual base of ontologies and knowledge representation which are often enriched by deeper and newer analysis. In this context, each language foregrounds specific features or nodes within this knowledge base by usually non-uniform means.

At the same time, the arrival of the age of Big Data has attracted extensive studies on the actual and dynamic use of language as contextualized (ala. Jakobson 1960) within a given society, especially through the mass media. What are foregrounded in this medium tend to have graded cognitive saliency characterizing members of the common speech community, and such shared knowledge is usually at great variance with the thesaurus approach and show noticeable localized features. It is proposed here that the two kinds of knowledge (thesauric vs cognitive-cultural) complement each other in human cognition, and are integral to it.

We draw on two large Chinese media databases Sketch (2.1 billion character tokens[1]) and LIVAC (550 million character tokens[2]) for illustration and discussion. The Sketch Engine in Chinese shows how ***apple*** is, as expected, primarily related to ***orange***, ***peach***, ***fruit***, ***vegetable***, ***food*** etc. At the same time three sub-corpora of LIVAC we draw on show that ***apple*** has a different set of saliency linkage with ***computer***, ***iPhone***, ***Jobs***, ***roll out***, ***share price***, ***company*** etc. This linkage is related less to the universalistic semantic network for ***apple***, than to the foregrounded awareness of ***apple*** as a cultural artifact in actual human social interaction and encoded as social knowledge (Park 1955, Longino 1990). We also show and examine how the salient information associated with ***apple*** varies across the three major Chinese speech communities: Beijing, Hong Kong and Taipei, reflecting social and societal differences, and regional developments, as well as variations over time. Similarly ***free-freedom*** in Chinese varies in associated saliency linkage in the three speech communities in interesting ways but also contrasts with the Sketch Engine results.

The above comparison in LIVAC is made possible by rigorous improvement to the common and simplistic approach to the cultivation and use of databases. The augmentation efforts included the rigorous cultivation of 3 comparable (sub-) corpora for Beijing, Hong Kong and Taipei through geographical (*horizontal*), chronological (*vertical*) and domain (*topical*) partitioning of what is often assumed to be a common linguistic database. This partitioning required well-reasoned pre-conceived criteria to ensure adequate equivalency in comparability in terms of size, period and depth of analysis.

To facilitate comparison we propose a Cognitive-cultural Salience Index (CSI) which draws on comparable corpus data (e.g. LIVAC) to provide comparison of the relative saliency of target words in the relevant corpus and presented as word clouds. The results are viewed in the light of the Sketch Engine output

[1]As per Sketch Engine website.
[2]As per LIVAC website.

Invited Paper Proceedings of the Eighth Workshop on Building and Using Comparable Corpora, pages 1–2,
Beijing, China, July 30, 2015.

to explore how our appreciation of knowledge representation may be enhanced. It will also serve to echo the call to optimize our data collection efforts and to broaden our queries with data judiciously curated and cultivated.

References

K. E. Boulding. 1956. *The image: Knowledge in life and sociology.* University of Michigan Press, Ann Arbor, MI.

C. R. Huang, A. Kilgarriff, Y. Wu, C. M. Chiu, S. Smith, P. Rychly, and K. J. Chen. 2005. Chinese Sketch Engine and the extraction of grammatical collocations. In *Proceedings of the Fourth SIGHAN Workshop on Chinese Language Processing*, pages 48–55.

R Jakobson. 1960. Closing statement: Linguistics and poetics. In T. Sebeok, editor, *Style in Language.*

A. Kilgarriff, V. Baisa, J. Bušta, M. Jakubíček, Kovář V., J. Michelfeit, P. Rychlý, and Suchomel V. 2014. The Sketch Engine: Ten years on. *Lexicography: Journal of ASIALEX*, 1(1):7–36.

Livac. `http://www.livac.org`; `https://en.wikipedia.org/wiki/LIVAC_Synchronous_Corpus`.

H. E. Longino. 1990. *Science and social knowledge: Values and objectivity in scientific inquiry.* Princeton University Press, Princeton, NJ.

R. E. Park. 1955. *Society: Collective behavior, news and opinion, sociology and modern society.* The Free Press, Glencoe, IL.

Sketch engine. `https://the.sketchengine.co.uk`; `https://en.wikipedia.org/wiki/Sketch_Engine`.

B. Tsou and O. Kwong. 2015. LIVAC as a monitoring corpus for tracking trends beyond linguistics. In B. K. Tsou and O. K. Kwong, editors, *Linguistic Corpus and Corpus Linguistics in the Chinese Context*, number 25 in Journal of Chinese Linguistics Monograph Series, pages 447–471, Hong Kong. Hong Kong Chinese University Press.

A Factory of Comparable Corpora from Wikipedia

Alberto Barrón-Cedeño[1], **Cristina España-Bonet**[2], **Josu Boldoba**[2] and **Lluís Màrquez**[1]
[1] Qatar Computing Research Institute, HBKU, Doha, Qatar
[2] TALP Research Center, Univesitat Politècnica de Catalunya, Barcelona, Spain
{albarron,lmarquez}@qf.org.qa
cristinae@cs.upc.edu jboldoba08@gmail.com

Abstract

Multiple approaches to grab comparable data from the Web have been developed up to date. Nevertheless, coming out with a high-quality comparable corpus of a specific topic is not straightforward. We present a model for the automatic extraction of comparable texts in multiple languages and on specific topics from Wikipedia. In order to prove the value of the model, we automatically extract parallel sentences from the comparable collections and use them to train statistical machine translation engines for specific domains. Our experiments on the English–Spanish pair in the domains of Computer Science, Science, and Sports show that our in-domain translator performs significantly better than a generic one when translating in-domain Wikipedia articles. Moreover, we show that these corpora can help when translating out-of-domain texts.

1 Introduction

Multilingual corpora with different levels of comparability are useful for a range of natural language processing (NLP) tasks. Comparable corpora were first used for extracting parallel lexicons (Rapp, 1995; Fung, 1995). Later they were used for feeding statistical machine translation (SMT) systems (Uszkoreit et al., 2010) and in multilingual retrieval models (Schönhofen et al., 2007; Potthast et al., 2008). SMT systems estimate the statistical models from bilingual texts (Koehn, 2010). Since only the words that appear in the corpus can be translated, having a corpus of the right domain is important to have high coverage. However, it is evident that no large collections of parallel texts for all domains and language pairs exist. In some cases, only general-domain parallel corpora are available; in some others there are no parallel resources at all.

One of the main sources of parallel data is the Web: websites in multiple languages are crawled and contents retrieved to obtain multilingual data. Wikipedia, an on-line community-curated encyclopædia with editions in multiple languages, has been used as a source of data for these purposes — for instance, (Adafre and de Rijke, 2006; Potthast et al., 2008; Otero and López, 2010; Plamada and Volk, 2012). Due to its encyclopædic nature, editors aim at organising its content within a dense taxonomy of categories.[1] Such a taxonomy can be exploited to extract comparable and parallel corpora on specific topics and knowledge domains. This allows to study how different topics are analysed in different languages, extract multilingual lexicons, or train specialised machine translation systems, just to mention some instances. Nevertheless, the process is not straightforward. The community-generated nature of the Wikipedia has produced a reasonably good —yet chaotic— taxonomy in which categories are linked to each other at will, even if sometimes no relationship among them exists, and the borders dividing different areas are far from being clearly defined.

The rest of the paper is distributed as follows. We briefly overview the definition of comparability levels in the literature and show the difficulties inherent to extracting comparable corpora from Wikipedia (Section 2). We propose a simple and effective platform for the extraction of comparable corpora from Wikipedia (Section 3). We describe a simple model for the extraction of parallel sentences from comparable corpora (Section 4). Experimental results are reported on each of these sub-tasks for three domains using the English and Spanish Wikipedia editions. We present an application-oriented evaluation of the comparable corpora by studying the impact of the extracted parallel sentences on a statistical machine translation system (Section 5). Finally, we draw conclusions and outline ongoing work (Section 6).

[1] http://en.wikipedia.org/wiki/Help:Category

Long Paper Proceedings of the Eighth Workshop on Building and Using Comparable Corpora, pages 3–13,
Beijing, China, July 30, 2015.

2 Background

Comparability in multilingual corpora is a fuzzy concept that has received alternative definitions without reaching an overall consensus (Rapp, 1995; Eagles Document Eag–Tcwg–Ctyp, 1996; Fung, 1998; Fung and Cheung, 2004; Wu and Fung, 2005; McEnery and Xiao, 2007; Sharoff et al., 2013). Ideally, a comparable corpus should contain texts in multiple languages which are similar in terms of *form* and *content*. Regarding content, they should observe similar structure, function, and a long list of characteristics: register, field, tenor, mode, time, and dialect (Maia, 2003).

Nevertheless, finding these characteristics in real-life data collections is virtually impossible. Therefore, we attach to the following simpler four-class classification (Skadiņa et al., 2010): (*i*) *Parallel texts* are true and accurate translations or approximate translations with minor language-specific variations. (*ii*) *Strongly comparable texts* are closely related texts reporting the same event or describing the same subject. (*iii*) *Weakly comparable texts* include texts in the same narrow subject domain and genre, but describing different events, as well as texts within the same broader domain and genre, but varying in sub-domains and specific genres. (*iv*) *Non-comparable texts* are pairs of texts drawn at random from a pair of very large collections of texts in two or more languages.

Wikipedia is a particularly suitable source of multilingual text with different levels of comparability, given that it covers a large amount of languages and topics.[2] Articles can be connected via interlanguage links (i.e., a link from a page in one Wikipedia language to an *equivalent* page in another language). Although there are some missing links and an article can be linked by two or more articles from the same language (Hecht and Gergle, 2010), the number of available links allows to exploit the multilinguality of Wikipedia.

Still, extracting a comparable corpus on a specific domain from Wikipedia is not so straightforward. One can take advantage of the user-generated categories associated to most articles. Ideally, the categories and sub-categories would compose a hierarchically organized taxonomy, e.g., in the form of a category tree. Nevertheless,

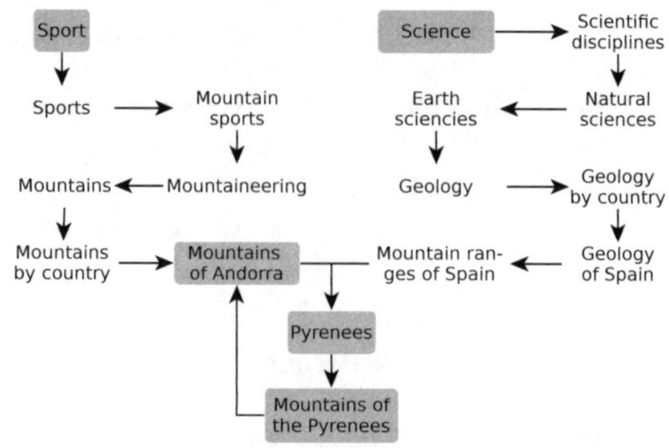

Figure 1: Slice of the Spanish Wikipedia category graph (as in May 2015) departing from categories `Sport` and `Science`. Translated for clarity.

the categories in Wikipedia compose a densely-connected graph with highly overlapping categories, cycles, etc. As they are manually-crafted, the categories are somehow arbitrary and, among other consequences, the potential categorisation of articles does not accomplish with the properties for representing the desirable —trusty enough— categorisation of articles from different domains. Moreover, many articles are not associated to the categories they should belong to and there is a phenomenon of over-categorization.[3]

Figure 1 is an example of the complexity of Wikipedia's category graph topology. Although this particular example comes from the Wikipedia in Spanish, similar phenomena exist in other editions. Firstly, the paths from different *apparently* unrelated categories —`Sport` and `Science`—, converge in a common node soon in the graph (node `Pyrenees`). As a result, not only `Pyrenees` could be considered as a sub-category of both `Sport` and `Science`, but all its descendants. Secondly, cycles exist among the different categories, as in the sequence `Mountains of Andorra` → `Pyrenees` → `Mountains of the Pyrenees` → `Mountains of Andorra`. Ideally, every sub-category of a category should share the same attributes, since the "failure to observe this principle reduces the predictability [of the taxonomy] and can lead to cross-classification" (Rowley and Hartley, 2000, p. 196). Although fixing this issue —inherent to all the Wikipedia editions— falls

[2]Wikipedia contains 288 language editions out of which 277 are active and 12 have more than 1M articles at the time of writing, June 2015 (`http://en.wikipedia.org/wiki/List_of_Wikipedias`).

[3]This is a phenomenon specially stressed in the Wikipedia itself: `http://en.wikipedia.org/wiki/Wikipedia:Overcategorization`.

out of the scope of our research, some heuristic strategies are necessary to diminish their impact in the domain definition process.

Plamada and Volk (2012) dodge this issue by extracting a domain comparable corpus using IR techniques. They use the characteristic vocabulary of the domain (100 terms extracted from an external in-domain corpus) to query a Lucene search engine[4] over the whole encyclopædia. Our approach is completely different: we try to get along with Wikipedia's structure with a strategy to walk through the category graph departing from a root or *pseudo-root* category, which defines our domain of interest. We empirically set a threshold to stop exploring the graph such that the included categories most likely represent an entire domain (cf. Section 3). This approach is more similar to Cui et al. (2008), who explore the *Wiki-Graph* and score every category in order to assess its likelihood of belonging to the domain.

Other tools are being developed to extract corpora from Wikipedia. Linguatools[5] released a comparable corpus extracted from Wikipedias in 253 language pairs. Unfortunately, neither their tool nor the applied methodology description are available. CatScan2[6] is a tool that allows to explore and search categories recursively. The Accurat toolkit (Pinnis et al., 2012; Ştefănescu, Dan and Ion, Radu and Hunsicker, Sabine, 2012)[7] aligns comparable documents and extracts parallel sentences, lexicons, and named entities. Finally, the most related tool to ours: CorpusPedia[8] extracts non-aligned, softly-aligned, and strongly-aligned comparable corpora from Wikipedia (Otero and López, 2010). The difference with respect to our model is that they only consider the articles associated to one specific category and not to an entire domain.

The inter-connection among Wikipedia editions in different languages has been exploited for multiple tasks including lexicon induction (Erdmann et al., 2008), extraction of bilingual dictionaries (Yu and Tsujii, 2009), and identification of particular translations (Chu et al., 2014; Prochasson and Fung, 2011). Different cross-language NLP tasks have particularly taken advantage of Wikipedia. Articles have been used for query translation (Schönhofen et al., 2007) and cross-language semantic representations for similarity estimation (Cimiano et al., 2009; Potthast et al., 2008; Sorg and Cimiano, 2012). The extraction of parallel corpora from Wikipedia has been a hot topic during the last years (Adafre and de Rijke, 2006; Patry and Langlais, 2011; Plamada and Volk, 2012; Smith et al., 2010; Tomás et al., 2008; Yasuda and Sumita, 2008).

3 Domain-Specific Comparable Corpora Extraction

In this section we describe our proposal to extract domain-specific comparable corpora from Wikipedia. The input to the pipeline is the top category of the domain (e.g., `Sport`). The terminology used in this description is as follows. Let c be a Wikipedia category and c^* be the top category of a domain. Let a be a Wikipedia article; $a \in c$ if a contains c among its categories. Let G be the Wikipedia category graph.

Vocabulary definition. The domain vocabulary represents the set of terms that better characterises the domain. We do not expect to have at our disposal the vocabulary associated to every category. Therefore, we build it from the Wikipedia itself. We collect every article $a \in c^*$ and apply standard pre-processing; i.e., tokenisation, stopwording, numbers and punctuation marks filtering, and stemming (Porter, 1980). In order to reduce noise, tokens shorter than four characters are discarded as well. The vocabulary is then composed of the top n terms, ranked by term frequency. This value is empirically determined.

Graph exploration. The input for this step is G, c^* (i.e., the departing node in the graph), and the domain vocabulary. Departing from c^*, we perform a breadth-first search, looking for all those categories which more likely belong to the required domain. Two constraints are applied in order to make a controlled exploration of the graph: (*i*) in order to avoid loops and exploring already traversed paths, a node can only be visited once, (*ii*) in order to avoid exploring the whole categories graph, a stopping criterion is pre-defined. Our stopping criterion is inspired by the classification tree-breadth first search algorithm (Cui et al., 2008). The core idea is scoring the explored cate-

[4] https://lucene.apache.org/

[5] http://linguatools.org

[6] http://tools.wmflabs.org/catscan2/catscan2.php

[7] http://www.accurat-project.eu

[8] http://gramatica.usc.es/pln/tools/CorpusPedia.html

Edition	Articles	Categories	Ratio
English	4,123,676	1,032,222	4.0
Spanish	965,543	210,803	4.6
Intersection	631,710	107,313	–

Table 1: Amount of articles and categories in the Wikipedia editions and in the intersection (i.e., pages linked across languages).

gories to determine if they belong to the domain. Our heuristic assumes that a category belongs to the domain if its title contains at least one of the terms in the characteristic vocabulary. Nevertheless, many categories exist that may not include any of the terms in the vocabulary. (e.g., consider category `pato` in Spanish —literally "duck" in English— which, somehow surprisingly, refers to a sport rather than an animal). Our naïve solution to this issue is to consider subsets of categories according to their depth respect to the root. An entire level of categories is considered part of the domain if a minimum percentage of its elements include vocabulary terms.

In our experiments we use the English and Spanish Wikipedia editions.[9] Table 1 shows some statistics, after filtering disambiguation and redirect pages. The intersection of articles and categories between the two languages represents the ceiling for the amount of parallel corpora one can gather for this pair. We focus on three domains: Computer Science (CS), Science (Sc), and Sports (Sp) —the top categories c^* from which the graph is explored in order to extract the corresponding comparable corpora.

Table 2 shows the number of *root articles* associated to c^* for each domain and language. From them, we obtain domain vocabularies with a size between 100 and 400 lemmas (right-side columns) when using the top 10% terms. We ran experiments using the top 10%, 15%, 20% and 100%. The relatively small size of these vocabularies allows to manually check that 10% is the best option to characterise the desired category, higher percentages add more noise than in-domain terms. The plots in Figure 2 show the percentage of categories with at least one domain term in the title: the starting point for our graph-based method for selecting the in-domain articles. As expected, nearly 100% of the categories in the root include domain terms and this percentage decreases with increasing depth in the tree.

[9]Dumps downloaded from `https://dumps.wikimedia.org` in July 2013 and pre-processed with JWPL (Zesch et al., 2008) (`https://code.google.com/p/jwpl/`).

	Articles		Vocabulary	
	en	es	en	es
CS	4	130	106	447
Sc	29	3	464	140
Sp	3	10	122	100

Table 2: Number of articles in the root categories and size of the resulting domain vocabulary.

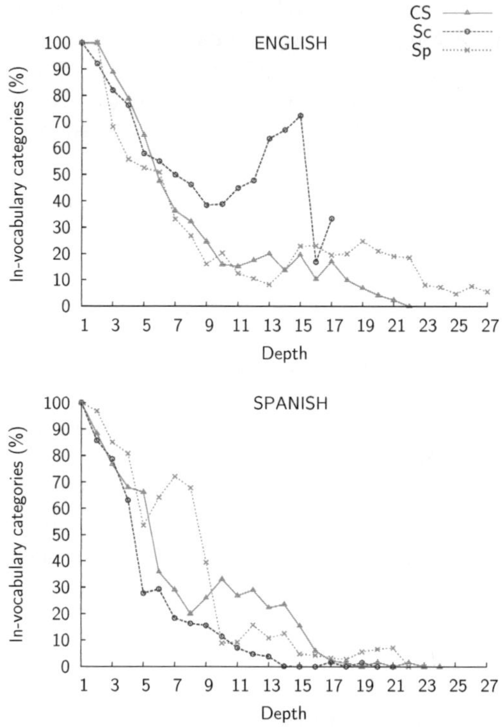

Figure 2: Percentage of categories with at least one domain term in the title for the two languages and the three domains under study.

When extracting the corpus, one must decide the adequate percentage of positive categories allowed. High thresholds lead to small corpora whereas low thresholds lead to larger —but noisier— corpora. As in many applications, this is a trade-off between precision and recall and depends on the intended use of the corpus. Table 3 shows some numbers on two different thresholds. Increasing the threshold does not always mean

	Articles		Distance from the root			
	50%	60%	50%		60%	
	en-es	en-es	en	es	en	es
CS	18,168	8,251	6	5	5	5
Sc	161,130	21,459	6	4	4	4
Sp	72,315	1,980	8	8	3	4

Table 3: Number of article pairs according to the percentage of positive categories used to select the levels of the graph and distance from the root at which the percentage is smaller to the desired one.

lowering the selected depth, but when it does, the difference in the number of extracted articles can be significant. The same table shows the number of article pairs extracted for each value: the resulting comparable corpus for each domain. The stopping level is selected for every language independently, but in order to reduce noise, the comparable corpus is only built from those articles that appear in both languages and are related via an interlanguage link. We validate the quality in terms of application-based utility of the generated comparable corpora when used in a translation system (cf. Section 5). Therefore, we choose to give more importance to recall and opt for the corpora obtained with a threshold of 50%.

4 Parallel Sentence Extraction

In this section we describe a simple technique for extracting parallel sentences from a comparable corpus.

Given a pair of articles related by an interlanguage link, we estimate the similarity between all their pairs of cross-language sentences with different text similarity measures. We repeat the process for all the pairs of articles and rank the resulting sentence pairs according to its similarity. After defining a threshold for each measure, those sentence pairs with a similarity higher than the threshold are extracted as parallel sentences. This is a non-supervised method that generates a noisy parallel corpus. The quality of the similarity measures will then affect the purity of the parallel corpus and, therefore, the quality of the translator. However, we do not need to be very restrictive with the measures here and still favour a large corpus, since the word alignment process in the SMT system can take care of part of the noise.

Similarity computation. We compute similarities between pairs of sentences by means of cosine and length factor measures. The cosine similarity is calculated on three well-known characterisations in cross-language information retrieval and parallel corpora alignment: (*i*) character n-grams (cng) (McNamee and Mayfield, 2004); (*ii*) pseudo-cognates (cog) (Simard et al., 1992); and (*iii*) word 1-grams, after translation into a common language, both from English to Spanish and vice versa (mono_{en}, mono_{es}). We add the (*iv*) length factor (len) (Pouliquen et al., 2003) as an independent measure and as penalty (multiplicative factor) on the cosine similarity.

The threshold for each of the measures just introduced is empirically set in a manually annotated corpus. We define it as the value that maximises the F_1 score on this development set. To create this set, we manually annotated a corpus with 30 article pairs (10 per domain) at sentence level. We considered three sentence classes: parallel, comparable, and other. The volunteers of the exercise were given as guidelines the definitions by Skadiņa et al. (2010) of *parallel text* and *strongly comparable text* (cf. Section 2). A pair that did not match any of these definitions had to be classified as other. Each article pair was annotated by two volunteers, native speakers of Spanish with high command of English (a total of nine volunteers participated in the process). The mean agreement between annotators had a kappa coefficient (Cohen, 1960) of $\kappa \sim 0.7$. A third annotator resolved disagreed sentences.[10]

Table 4 shows the thresholds that obtain the maximum F_1 scores. It is worth noting that, even if the values of precision and recall are relatively low —the maximum recall is 0.57 for len—, our intention with these simple measures is not to obtain the highest performance in terms of retrieval, but injecting the most useful data to the translator, even at the cost of some noise. The performance with character 3-grams is the best one, comparable to that of mono, with an F_1 of 0.36. This suggests that a translator is not mandatory for performing the sentences selection. Len and 1-grams have no discriminating power and lead to the worse scores (F_1 of 0.14 and 0.21, respectively).

We ran a second set of experiments to explore the combination of the measures. Table 5 shows

[10]The corpus is publicly available at `http://www.cs.upc.edu/~cristinae/CV/recursos.php`.

	c1g	c2g	c3g	c4g	c5g	cog	$mono_{en}$	$mono_{es}$	len
Thres.	0.95	0.60	0.25	0.20	0.15	0.30	0.20	0.15	0.90
P	0.18	0.29	0.28	0.24	0.23	0.16	0.30	0.26	0.08
R	0.25	0.31	0.53	0.47	0.47	0.49	0.46	0.34	0.57
F_1	0.21	0.30	0.36	0.32	0.31	0.24	0.36	0.30	0.14

Table 4: Best thresholds and their associated Precision (P), recall (R) and F_1.

	$\bar{S}$	$\bar{S}$·len	$\overline{S \cdot F_1}$	$\overline{S \cdot F_1}$·len
Thres.	0.25	0.15	0.05	0.05
P	0.27	0.33	0.18	0.32
R	0.50	0.62	0.77	0.65
F_1	0.35	0.43	0.29	0.43

Table 5: Precision, recall, and F_1 for the average of the similarities weighted by length model (len) and/or their F_1.

	CS	Sc	Sp
c1g	207,592	1,585,582	404,656
c2g	99,964	745,821	326,882
c3g	96,039	724,210	335,147
c4g	110,701	863,090	394,105
c5g	126,692	1,012,993	466,007
cog	182,981	1,215,008	451,941
len	271,073	1,941,866	550,338
$mono_{en}$	211,209	1,367,917	461,731
$mono_{es}$	183,439	1,273,509	435,671
$\bar{S}$	154,917	1,098,453	450,933
$\bar{S}$·len	121,697	957,662	390,783
$\overline{S \cdot F_1}$	153,056	1,085,502	448,076
$\overline{S \cdot F_1}$·len	121,407	957,967	392,241

Table 6: Size of the parallel corpora extracted with each similarity measure.

the performance obtained by averaging all the similarities ($\bar{S}$), also after multiplying them by the length factor and/or the observed F_1 obtained in the previous experiment. Even if the length factor had shown a poor performance in isolation, it helps to lift the F_1 figures consistently after affecting the similarities. In this case, F_1 grows up to 0.43. This impact is not so relevant when the individual F_1 is used for weighting $\bar{S}$.

We applied all the measures —both combined and in isolation— on the entire comparable corpora previously extracted. Table 6 shows the amount of parallel sentences extracted by applying the empirically defined thresholds of Tables 4 and 5. As expected, more flexible alternatives, such as low-level n-grams or length factor result in a higher amount of retrieved instances, but in all cases the size of the corpora is remarkable. For the most restricted domain, CS, we get around 200k parallel sentences for a given similarity measure. For the widest domain, SC, we surpass the 1M sentence pairs. As it will be shown in the following section, these sizes are already useful to be used for training SMT systems. Some standard parallel corpora have the same order of magnitude. For tasks other than MT, where the precision on the extracted pairs can be more important than the recall, one can obtain cleaner corpora by using a threshold that maximises precision instead of F_1.

5 Evaluation: Statistical Machine Translation Task

In this section we validate the quality of the obtained corpora by studying its impact on statistical machine translation. There are several parallel corpora for the English–Spanish language pair. We select as a general-purpose corpus Europarl v7 (Koehn, 2005), with 1.97M parallel sentences. The order of magnitude is similar to the largest corpus we have extracted from Wikipedia, so we can compare the results in a size-independent way. If our corpus extracted from Wikipedia was made up with parallel fragments of the desired domain, it should be the most adequate to translate these domains. If the quality of the parallel fragments was acceptable, it should also help when translating out-of-domain texts. In order to test these hypotheses we analyse three settings: (*i*) train SMT systems only with Wikipedia (WP) *or* Europarl (EP) to translate domain-specific texts, (*ii*) train SMT systems with Wikipedia *and* Europarl to translate domain-specific texts, and (*iii*) train SMT systems with Wikipedia *and* Europarl to translate out-of-domain texts (news).

For the out-of-domain evaluation we use the News Commentaries 2011 test set and the News Commentaries 2009 for development.[11] For the in-domain evaluation we build the test and development sets in a semiautomatic way. We depart from the parallel corpora gathered in Section 4 from which sentences with more than four tokens and beginning with a letter are selected. We estimate its perplexity with respect to a language model obtained with Europarl in order to select the most fluent sentences and then we rank the parallel sentences according to their similarity and perplexity. The top-n fragments were manually revised and extracted to build the Wikipedia test (WPtest) and development (WPdev) sets. We repeated the process for the three studied domains and drew 300 parallel fragments for development for every domain and 500 for test. We removed these sentences from the corresponding training corpora. For one of the domains, CS, we also gathered a test set from a parallel corpus of GNOME localisation files (Tiedemann, 2012). Table 7 shows the size in number of sentences of these test sets and of the 20 Wikipedia training sets used for translation. Only one measure, that with the highest F_1 score, is selected from each family: c3g, cog, mono$_{en}$ and $\bar{S}$·len (cf. Tables 4 and 5). We also compile the corpus that results from the union of the previous four. Notice that, although we eliminate duplicates from this corpus, the size of the union is close to the sum of the individual corpora. This indicates that every similarity measure selects a different set of parallel fragments. Beside the specialised corpus for each domain, we build a larger corpus with all the data (Un). Again, duplicate fragments coming from articles belonging to more than one domain are removed.

SMT systems are trained using standard freely available software. We estimate a 5-gram language model using interpolated Kneser–Ney discounting with SRILM (Stolcke, 2002). Word alignment is done with GIZA++ (Och and Ney, 2003) and both phrase extraction and decoding are done with Moses (Koehn et al., 2007). We optimise the feature weights of the model with Minimum Error Rate Training (MERT) (Och, 2003) against the BLEU evaluation metric (Papineni et al., 2002). Our model considers the language model, direct and inverse phrase probabilities, direct and inverse lexical probabilities, phrase and word penalties, and a lexicalised reordering.

[11]Both are available at http://www.statmt.org/wmt14/translation-task.html.

	CS	Sc	Sp	Un
c3g	95,715	723,760	334,828	883,366
cog	182,283	1,213,965	451,324	1,430,962
mono$_{en}$	210,664	1,367,169	461,237	1,638,777
$\bar{S}$·len	120,835	956,346	389,975	1,160,977
union	577,428	3,847,381	1,181,664	4,948,241
WPdev	300	300	300	900
WPtest	500	500	500	1500
GNOME	1000	–	–	–

Table 7: Number of sentences of the Wikipedia parallel corpora used to train the SMT systems (top rows) and of the sets used for development and test.

	CS	Sc	Sp	Un	Comp.
Europarl	27.99	34.00	30.02	30.63	–
c3g	38.81	40.53	46.94	43.68	43.68
cog	57.32	56.17	57.60	58.14	54.89
mono$_{en}$	54.27	52.96	55.74	55.17	52.45
$\bar{S}$·len	56.14	57.40	58.39	58.80	56.78
union	**64.65**	**62.95**	**62.65**	**64.47**	–

Table 8: BLEU scores obtained on the Wikipedia test sets for the 20 specialised systems described in Section 5. A comparison column (Comp.) where all the systems are trained with corpora of the same size is also included (see text).

(*i*) Training systems with Wikipedia *or* Europarl for domain-specific translation. Table 8 shows the evaluation results on WPtest. All the specialised systems obtain significant improvements with respect to the Europarl system, regardless of their size. For instance, the worst specialised system (c3g with only 95,715 sentences for CS) outperforms by more than 10 points of BLEU the general Europarl translator. The most complete system (the union of the four representatives) doubles the BLEU score for all the domains with an impressive improvement of 30 points. This is of course possible due to the nature of the test set that has been extracted from the same collection as the training data and therefore shares its structure and vocabulary.

To give perspective to these high numbers we evaluate the systems trained on the CS domain

	CS	Un	Comp.
c3g	11.08	9.56	9.56
cog	18.48	17.66	16.31
mono$_{en}$	19.48	20.58	18.84
$\bar{S}$·len	20.71	20.56	19.76
union	**22.41**	20.63	–

Table 9: BLEU scores obtained on the GNOME test set for systems trained only with Wikipedia. A system with Europarl achieves a score of 18.15.

against the GNOME dataset (Table 9). Except for c3g, the Wikipedia translators always outperform the baseline with EP; the union system improves it by 4 BLEU points (22.41 compared to 18.15) with a four times smaller corpus. This confirms that a corpus automatically extracted with an F_1 smaller than 0.5 is still useful for SMT. Notice also that using only the in-domain data (CS) is always better than using the whole WP corpus (Un) even if the former is in general ten times smaller (cf. Table 7).

According to this indirect evaluation of the similarity measures, character n-grams (c3g) represent the worst alternative. These results contradict the direct evaluation, where c3g and mono$_{en}$ had the highest F_1 scores on the development set among the individual similarity measures. The size of the corpus is not relevant here: when we train all the systems with the same amount of data, the ranking in the quality of the measures remains the same. To see this, we trained four additional systems with the top m number of parallel fragments, where m is the size of the smallest corpus for the union of domains: Un-c3g. This new comparison is reported in columns "Comp." in Tables 8 and 9. In this fair comparison c3g is still the worst measure and S̄·len the best one. The translator built from its associated corpus outperforms with less than half of the data used for training the general one (883,366 vs. 1,965,734 parallel fragments) both in WPtest (56.78 vs. 30.63) and GNOME (19.76 vs. 18.15).

***(ii)* Training systems on Wikipedia *and* Europarl for domain-specific translation.** Now we enrich the general translator with Wikipedia data or, equivalently, complement the Wikipedia translator with out-of-domain data. Table 10 shows the results. Augmenting the size of the in-domain corpus by 2 million fragments improves the results even more, about 2 points of BLEU

	CS	Sc	Sp	Un
Europarl	27.99	34.00	30.02	30.63
union	64.65	62.95	62.65	64.47
EP+c3g	46.07	48.29	50.40	49.34
EP+cog	58.39	57.70	59.05	58.98
EP+mono$_{en}$	54.44	53.93	56.05	55.88
EP+$\bar{S}$·len	56.05	57.53	59.78	58.72
EP+union	**66.22**	**64.24**	**64.39**	**65.67**

Table 10: BLEU scores obtained on the Wikipedia test set for the 20 systems trained with the combination of the Europarl (EP) and the Wikipedia corpora. The results with a Europarl system and the best one from Table 8 (union) shown for comparison.

	CS	Un
EP+c3g	19.78	19.49
EP+cog	21.09	20.14
EP+mono$_{en}$	21.27	20.66
EP+$\bar{S}$·len	21.58	20.65
EP+union	**22.37**	21.43

Table 11: BLEU scores obtained on the GNOME test set for systems trained with Europarl and Wikipedia. A system with Europarl achieves a score of 18.15.

when using all the union data. System c3g benefits the most of the inclusion of the Europarl data. The reason is that it is the individual system with less corpus available and the one obtaining the worst results. In fact, the better the Wikipedia system, the less important the contribution from Europarl is. For the independent test set GNOME, Table 11 shows that the union corpus on CS is better than any combination of Wikipedia and Europarl. Still, as aforementioned, the best performance on this test set is obtained with a pure in-domain system (cf. Table 9).

***(iii)* Training systems on Wikipedia and Europarl for out-of-domain translation.** Now we check the performance of the Wikipedia translators on the out-of-domain news test. Table 12 shows the results. In this neutral domain for Europarl and Wikipedia, the in-domain Wikipedia systems show a lower performance. The BLEU score obtained with the Europarl system is 27.02 whereas the Wikipedia union system achieves 22.16. When combining the two corpora, results

	CS	Sc	Sp	Un
union	16.74	22.28	15.82	22.16
EP+c3g	26.06	26.35	26.81	**27.07**
EP+cog	26.61	**27.33**	26.71	**27.08**
EP+mono$_{en}$	**27.18**	26.80	26.96	**27.44**
EP+$\bar{S}$·len	**27.59**	26.80	**27.58**	**27.22**
EP+union	26.76	**27.52**	**27.35**	26.72

Table 12: BLEU scores for the out-of-domain evaluation on the News Commentaries 2011 test set. We show in boldface all the systems that improve the Europarl translator, which achieves a score of 27.02.

are controlled by the Europarl baseline. In general, systems in which we include only texts from an unrelated domain do not improve the performance of the Europarl system alone, results of the combined system are better when we use Wikipedia texts from all the domains together (column Un) for training. This suggests that, as expected, a general Wikipedia corpus is necessary to build a general translator. This is a different problem to deal with.

6 Conclusions and Ongoing Work

In this paper we presented a model for the automatic extraction of in-domain comparable corpora from Wikipedia. It makes possible the automatic extraction of monolingual and comparable article collections as well as a one-click parallel corpus generation for on-demand language pairs and domains. Given a pair of languages and a main category, the model explores the Wikipedia categories graph and identifies a subset of categories (and their associated articles) to generate a document-aligned comparable corpus. The resulting corpus can be exploited for multiple natural language processing tasks. Here we applied it as part of a pipeline for the extraction of domain-specific parallel sentences. These parallel instances allowed for a significant improvement in the machine translation quality when compared to a generic system and applied to a domain specific corpus (in-domain). The experiments are shown for the English–Spanish language pair and the domains Computer Science, Science, and Sports. Still it can be applied to other language pairs and domains.

The prototype is currently operating in other languages. The only prerequisite is the existence of the corresponding Wikipedia edition and some basic processing tools such as a tokeniser and a lemmatiser. Our current efforts intend to generate a more robust model for parallel sentences identification and the design of other indirect evaluation schemes to validate the model performance.

Acknowledgments

This work was partially funded by the TACARDI project (TIN2012-38523-C02) of the Spanish Ministerio de Economía y Competitividad (MEC).

References

Sisay Fissaha Adafre and Maarten de Rijke. 2006. Finding Similar Sentences across Multiple Languages in Wikipedia. In *Proceedings of the 11th Conference of the European Chapter of the Association for Computational Linguistics*, pages 62–69.

Nicoletta Calzolari, Khalid Choukri, Bente Maegaard, Joseph Mariani, Jan Odjik, Stelios Piperidis, and Daniel Tapias, editors. 2008. *Proceedings of the Sixth International Language Resources and Evaluation (LREC 2008)*, Marrakech, Morocco. European Language Resources Association (ELRA).

Chenhui Chu, Toshiaki Nakazawa, and Sadao Kurohashi. 2014. Iterative Bilingual Lexicon Extraction from Comparable Corpora with Topical and Contextual Knowledge. In Alexander Gelbukh, editor, *Computational Linguistics and Intelligent Text Processing*, volume 8404 of *Lecture Notes in Computer Science*, pages 296–309. Springer Berlin Heidelberg.

Philipp Cimiano, Antje Schultz, Sergej Sizov, Philipp Sorg, and Steffen Staab. 2009. Explicit Versus Latent Concept Models for Cross-language Information Retrieval. In *Proceedings of the 21st International Jont Conference on Artifical Intelligence*, IJCAI'09, pages 1513–1518, San Francisco, CA, USA. Morgan Kaufmann Publishers Inc.

Jacob Cohen. 1960. A coefficient of agreement for nominal scales. *Educational and Psychological Measurement*, 20(1):37–46.

Gaoying Cui, Qin Lu, Wenjie Li, and Yirong Chen. 2008. Corpus Exploitation from Wikipedia for Ontology Construction. In Calzolari et al. (Calzolari et al., 2008), pages 2126–2128.

Eagles Document Eag–Tcwg–Ctyp. 1996. EAGLES Preliminary recommendations on Corpus Typology.

Maike Erdmann, Kotaro Nakayama, Takahiro Hara, and Shojiro Nishio. 2008. An Approach for Extracting Bilingual Terminology from Wikipedia. In

Proceedings of the 13th International Conference on Database Systems for Advanced Applications, DASFAA'08, pages 380–392, Berlin, Heidelberg. Springer-Verlag.

Pascale Fung and Percy Cheung. 2004. Mining verynon-parallel corpora: Parallel sentence and lexicon extraction via bootstrapping and em. In *Proceedings of EMNLP*, pages 57–63, Barcelona, Spain, July 25–July 26.

Pascale Fung. 1995. Compiling Bilingual Lexicon Entries from a Non-Parallel English-Chinese Corpus. In *Proceedings of the Third Annual Workshop on Very Large Corpora*, pages 173–183.

Pascale Fung. 1998. A Statistical View on Bilingual Lexicon Extraction: From Parallel Corpora to Non-Parallel Corpora. *Lecture Notes in Computer Science*, 1529:1–17.

Brent Hecht and Darren Gergle. 2010. The Tower of Babel Meets Web 2.0: User-generated Content and Its Applications in a Multilingual Context. In *Proceedings of the SIGCHI Conference on Human Factors in Computing Systems*, CHI '10, pages 291–300, New York, NY, USA. ACM.

Philipp Koehn, Hieu Hoang, Alexandra Birch, Chris Callison-Burch, Marcello Federico, Nicola Bertoldi, Brooke Cowan, Wade Shen, Christine Moran, Richard Zens, Chris Dyer, Ondrej Bojar, Alexandra Constantin, and Evan Herbst. 2007. Moses: Open Source Toolkit for Statistical Machine Translation. In *Proceedings of the 45th Annual Meeting of the Association for Computational Linguistics (ACL 2007)*, Prague, Czech Republic.

Philipp Koehn. 2005. Europarl: A Parallel Corpus for Statistical Machine Translation. In *Proceedings of the Machine Translation Summit X*, pages 79–86.

Philipp Koehn. 2010. *Statistical Machine Translation*. Cambridge University Press, New York, NY, USA, 1st edition.

Belinda Maia. 2003. What are comparable corpora. In *Proceedings of the Corpus Linguistics workshop on Multilingual Corpora: Linguistic requirements and technical perspectives*.

Anthony M. McEnery and Zhonghua Xiao, 2007. *Incorporating Corpora: Translation and the Linguist*, chapter Parallel and comparable corpora: What are they up to? Translating Europe. Multilingual Matters.

Paul McNamee and James Mayfield. 2004. Character N-Gram Tokenization for European Language Text Retrieval. *Information Retrieval*, 7(1-2):73–97.

Franz Josef Och and Hermann Ney. 2003. A Systematic Comparison of Various Statistical Alignment Models. *Computational Linguistics*, 29(1):19–51. See also [`http://www.fjoch.com/GIZA++.html`].

Franz Josef Och. 2003. Minimum Error Rate Training in Statistical Machine Translation. In *Proceedings of the 41st Annual Meeting of the Association for Computational Linguistics (ACL)*, pages 160–167, Sapporo, Japan.

Pablo Gamallo Otero and Issac González López. 2010. Wikipedia as multilingual source of comparable corpora. In *Proceedings of the 3rd Workshop on Building and Using Comparable Corpora*, pages 21–25, 22 May. Available at http://www.fb06.uni-mainz.de/lk/bucc2010/documents/Proceedings-BUCC-2010.pdf.

Kishore Papineni, Salim Roukos, Todd Ward, and Wei-Jing Zhu. 2002. BLEU: A Method for Automatic Evaluation of Machine Translation. In *Proceedings of the 40th Annual Meeting of the Association for Computational Linguistics (ACL 2002)*, pages 311–318, Philadelphia, PA. Association for Computational Linguistics.

Alexandre Patry and Philippe Langlais. 2011. Identifying Parallel Documents from a Large Bilingual Collection of Texts: Application to Parallel Article Extraction in Wikipedia. In Pierre Zweigenbaum, Reinhard Rapp, and Serge Sharoff, editors, *Proceedings of the 4th Workshop on Building and Using Comparable Corpora: Comparable Corpora and the Web*, pages 87–95, Portland, Oregon. Association for Computational Linguistics.

Mārcis Pinnis, Radu Ion, Dan Ştefănescu, Fangzhong Su, Inguna Skadiņa, Andrejs Vasiļjevs, and Bogdan Babych. 2012. Accurat toolkit for multi-level alignment and information extraction from comparable corpora. In *Proceedings of the ACL 2012 System Demonstrations*, ACL'12, pages 91–96, Stroudsburg, PA, USA. Association for Computational Linguistics.

Magdalena Plamada and Martin Volk. 2012. Towards a Wikipedia-extracted alpine corpus. In *The Fifth Workshop on Building and Using Comparable Corpora*, May.

Martin F. Porter. 1980. An Algorithm for Suffix Stripping. *Program*, 14:130–137.

Martin Potthast, Benno Stein, and Maik Anderka. 2008. A Wikipedia-Based Multilingual Retrieval Model. *Advances in Information Retrieval, 30th European Conference on IR Research*, LNCS (4956):522–530. Springer-Verlag.

Bruno Pouliquen, Ralf Steinberger, and Camelia Ignat. 2003. Automatic Identification of Document Translations in Large Multilingual Document Collections. In *Proceedings of the International Conference on Recent Advances in Natural Language Processing (RANLP-2003)*, pages 401–408, Borovets, Bulgaria.

Emmanuel Prochasson and Pascale Fung. 2011. Rare Word Translation Extraction from Aligned Comparable Documents. In *Proceedings of the 49th Annual*

Meeting of the Association for Computational Linguistics: Human Language Technologies - Volume 1, HLT '11, pages 1327–1335, Stroudsburg, PA, USA. Association for Computational Linguistics.

Reinhard Rapp. 1995. Identifying Word Translations in Non-Parallel Texts. *CoRR*, cmp-lg/9505037.

Jennifer Rowley and Richard Hartley. 2000. *Organizing Knowledge. An Introduction to Managing Access to Information*. Ashgate, 3rd edition.

Péter Schönhofen, András A. Benczúr, István Bíró, and Károly Csalogány. 2007. Cross-language retrieval with wikipedia. In *Advances in Multilingual and Multimodal Information Retrieval, 8th Workshop of the Cross-Language Evaluation Forum, CLEF 2007, Budapest, Hungary, September 19-21, 2007, Revised Selected Papers*, pages 72–79.

Serge Sharoff, Reinhard Rapp, and Pierre Zweigenbaum, 2013. *Building and Using Comparable Corpora*, chapter Overviewing Important Aspects of the Last Twenty Years of Research in Comparable Corpora. Springer.

Michel Simard, George F. Foster, and Pierre Isabelle. 1992. Using Cognates to Align Sentences in Bilingual Corpora. In *Proceedings of the Fourth International Conference on Theoretical and Methodological Issues in Machine Translation*.

Inguna Skadiņa, Ahmet Aker, Voula Giouli, Dan Tufiş, Robert Gaizauskas, Madara Mieriņa, and Nikos Mastropavlos. 2010. A collection of comparable corpora for under-resourced languages. In *Proceedings of the 2010 Conference on Human Language Technologies – The Baltic Perspective: Proceedings of the Fourth International Conference Baltic HLT 2010*, pages 161–168, Amsterdam, The Netherlands, The Netherlands. IOS Press.

Jason R. Smith, Chris Quirk, and Kristina Toutanova. 2010. Extracting Parallel Sentences from Comparable Corpora using Document Level Alignment. In *Human Language Technologies: The 2010 Annual Conference of the North American Chapter of the Association for Computational Linguistics*, HLT '10, pages 403–411, Stroudsburg, PA, USA. Association for Computational Linguistics.

Philipp Sorg and Philipp Cimiano. 2012. Exploiting Wikipedia for Cross-lingual and Multilingual Information Retrieval. *Data Knowl. Eng.*, 74:26–45, April.

Ştefănescu, Dan and Ion, Radu and Hunsicker, Sabine. 2012. Hybrid Parallel Sentence Mining from Comparable Corpora. In *Proceedings of the 16th Annual Conference of the European Association for Machine Translation (EAMT 2012)*, Trento, Italy. European Association for Machine Translation .

Andreas Stolcke. 2002. SRILM - An Extensible Language Modeling toolkit. In *Intl. Conference on Spoken Language Processing*, Denver, Colorado.

Jörg Tiedemann. 2012. Parallel Data, Tools and Interfaces in OPUS. In Nicoletta Calzolari, Khalid Choukri, Thierry Declerck, Mehmet Ugur Dogan, Bente Maegaard, Joseph Mariani, Jan Odijk, and Stelios Piperidis, editors, *Proceedings of the Eighth International Conference on Language Resources and Evaluation (LREC 2012)*, Istanbul, Turkey, May. European Language Resources Association (ELRA).

Jesús Tomás, Jordi Bataller, Francisco Casacuberta, and Jaime Lloret. 2008. Mining wikipedia as a parallel and comparable corpus. *LANGUAGE FORUM*, 34(1). Article presented at CICLing-2008, 9th International Conference on Intelligent Text Processing and Computational Linguistics, February 17 to 23, 2008, Haifa, Israel.

Jakob Uszkoreit, Jay Ponte, Ashok Popat, and Moshe Dubiner. 2010. Large scale parallel document mining for machine translation. In Chu-Ren Huang and Dan Jurafsky, editors, *Proceedings of the 23rd International Conference on Computational Linguistics (COLING 2010)*, pages 1101–1109, Beijing, China, August. COLING 2010 Organizing Committee.

Dekai Wu and Pascale Fung. 2005. Inversion transduction grammar constraints for mining parallel sentences from quasi-comparable corpora. In *Natural Language Processing - IJCNLP 2005, Second International Joint Conference*, pages 257–268, Jeju Island, Korea, Oct 11–Oct 13.

Keiji Yasuda and Eiichiro Sumita. 2008. Method for Building Sentence-Aligned Corpus from Wikipedia. In *Association for the Advancement of Artificial Intelligence*.

Kun Yu and Junichi Tsujii. 2009. Bilingual dictionary extraction from wikipedia. In *Proceedings of Machine Translation Summit XII*.

Torsten Zesch, Christof Müller, and Iryna Gurevych. 2008. Extracting Lexical Semantic Knowledge from Wikipedia and Wikictionary. In Calzolari et al. (Calzolari et al., 2008).

Knowledge-lean projection of coreference chains across languages

Yulia Grishina
Applied Computational Linguistics
University of Potsdam
grishina@uni-potsdam.de

Manfred Stede
Applied Computational Linguistics
University of Potsdam
stede@uni-potsdam.de

Abstract

Common technologies for automatic coreference resolution require either a language-specific rule set or large collections of manually annotated data, which is typically limited to newswire texts in major languages. This makes it difficult to develop coreference resolvers for a large number of the so-called low-resourced languages. We apply a direct projection algorithm on a multi-genre and multilingual corpus (English, German, Russian) to automatically produce coreference annotations for two target languages without exploiting any linguistic knowledge of the languages. Our evaluation of the projected annotations shows promising results, and the error analysis reveals structural differences of referring expressions and coreference chains for the three languages, which can now be targeted with more linguistically-informed projection algorithms.

1 Introduction

Coreference resolution requires relatively expensive resources, usually in terms of manual annotation. To alleviate this problem for low-resourced languages, techniques of annotation projection can be applied. In this paper, we report on experiments with projecting nominal coreference chains across bilingual corpora. Our goal is to see how well a knowledge-lean projection algorithm works for two relatively similar languages (English-German) and for less similar languages (English-Russian). Furthermore, we are interested in differences incurred by the text genre and therefore use three different genres: argumentative newspaper articles, narratives, and medicine instruction leaflets.

Our general aim is to explore the limitations of a knowledge-lean approach to the problem, so that it is easy to generalize to other low-resourced languages. For the annotation of the corpus, we created common annotation guidelines that make few assumptions on the structural features of the target languages. We used the guidelines to annotate texts of the three genres in the three languages, and provide results on inter-annotator agreement (see Section 3). For projection, we use a procedure based on sentence and word alignment as calculated by a standard tool (GIZA++) that was trained on corpora of moderate size. Thus at this point we deliberately do not apply linguistic knowledge on the languages involved. The experiments and results are described in Section 4. We present a qualitative error analysis showing that a number of structural divergences are responsible for many of the problems; this suggests that limited syntactic knowledge can be helpful for improving performance in follow-up work. Section 5 compares our results to the most closely related earlier work, and Section 6 concludes.

2 Related work

A *projection* approach is used to automatically transfer different types of linguistic annotation from one language to another. The idea of mapping from well-studied languages to low-resourced languages was initially introduced in the work of Yarowsky et al. (2001), who studied the induction of PoS and NE taggers, NP chunkers and morphological analyzers for different languages using annotation projection. Thereafter, the technique has been used for a variety of

Long Paper Proceedings of the Eighth Workshop on Building and Using Comparable Corpora, pages 14–22,
Beijing, China, July 30, 2015.

tasks, including PoS tagging and syntactic parsing (Hwa et al., 2005; Ozdowska, 2006; Tiedemann, 2014), semantic role labelling (Padó and Lapata, 2005), sentiment analysis (Mihalcea et al., 2007), mention detection (Zitouni and Florian, 2008), or named-entity recognition (Ehrmann et al., 2011).

To our knoweldge, the first application to coreference is due to Harabagiu and Maiorano (2000), who experimented with manually projecting coreference chains from English to Romanian using a translated parallel corpus. They showed that a coreference resolver trained on a parallel corpus can achieve better results than one trained on monolingual data. Then, Postolache and colleagues (2006) used automatic word alignment to project coreference annotations for the same data. Their goal was to achieve high precision, and thus they discarded from projection those referring expressions (henceforth: REs) whose syntactic heads were not properly aligned. Their results indeed show high precision (over 95%), but considerably lower recall (around 70%). We will discuss their approach in relation to ours in Section 5.

Mitkov and Barbu (2002) performed anaphora resolution using projection on a parallel English-French corpus, which lead to an improvement in the success rate of roughly 4% for both English and French. (Sayeed et al., 2009) used cross-lingual projection to improve the detection of coreferent named entities with the help of English-Arabic translations, and they reported better results than a monolingual resolver could achieve. (Rahman and Ng, 2012) used translation-based projection to train a coreference resolver, and achieved around 90% of the average F-scores of a supervised resolver in experiments with Spanish and Italian using few resources (only a mention extractor) for the target languages.

3 Multilingual coreference corpus

3.1 The corpus

Our corpus consists of 38 parallel texts in English, German and Russian, belonging to three genres: newswire articles (7 texts per language), short stories (3 texts per language), and medicine instruction leaflets (4 per language, only English-German)[1]. This choice is motivated by (i) the common observation that narrative texts are easier to process for coreference, (ii) the fact that news text is important for many applications, and (iii) the consideration of medical leaflets representing a somewhat "exotic" genre that exhibits many differences to the other two.

Corpus statistics are shown in Table 1. The stories contain more REs than the newswire texts, and the coreference chains of the stories tend to be much longer.

3.2 Annotation

Usually, coreference annotation guidelines have been designed with one target language in mind. In contrast, our goal was to have common guidelines for the three languages, in order to (i) obtain uniform nominal coreference annotations in our corpus (supporting the projection task), and (ii) facilitate extension to further languages. Regarding English, our guidelines are of similar length and quite compatible with the scheme used for OntoNotes - the largest annotated coreference corpus for the English language (Hovy et al., 2006). One exception is that we handle only NPs and do not annotate verbs that are coreferent with NPs.

Our guidelines borrow many decisions from the (relatively language-neutral) Potsdam Coreference Scheme (PoCoS) (Krasavina and Chiarcos, 2007), and we also considered the recently developed guidelines for thr English-German parallel corpus *ParCor* (Guillou et al., 2014). But it considers only pairwise annotation of anaphoric pronouns and their antecedents, whereas we annotate all REs appearing in a coreference chain (i.e. that are mentioned in the text at least twice).

For the time being, our annotation is restricted to the referential *identity*; we thus exclude cases of 'bridging' (also called 'indirect anaphora') or near-identity. The following types of REs are considered as markables: full NPs, proper names, and pronouns (personal, demonstrative, relative, reflexive, and pronominal adverbs). As in OntoNotes, generic nouns can corefer with definite full NPs or pronouns, but not with other generic nouns. In case of English nominal premodifiers, we only annotate a nominal premodifier if it can refer to a named entity (the $[US]_1$ politicians) or is an independent noun in the Genitive form ($[creditor's]_1$ choice); in all other cases,

[1]Newswire is taken from the multilingual newswire agency Project Syndicate (www.project-syndicate.org). Stories are taken from an online collection of parallel texts for second language acquisition (http://www.lonweb.org). Medical texts are from the EMEA subcorpus of the OPUS collection of parallel corpora (Tiedemann, 2009).

	Newswire			Stories			Medicine leaflets		Total		
	En	De	Ru	En	De	Ru	En	De	En	De	Ru
Tokens	5903	6268	5763	2619	2642	2343	3386	3002	11908	11912	8106
Sentences	239	252	239	190	186	192	160	160	589	598	431
REs	558	589	606	470	497	479	322	309	1350	1395	1085
Chains	124	140	140	45	45	48	90	88	259	273	188

Table 1: Statistics for the experimental corpus

nominal premodifiers are not annotated as separate markables (e.g., [bank account]).

When annotators identify a markable, they also record its RE type from an attribute menu. The markable span includes the syntactic head of the NP and all its modifiers, except for dependent relative clauses (because relative pronouns are treated as separate markables). As a divergence from OntoNotes, they have a separate relation for appositions, whereas we only include them in the head NP markable. Technically, we used the MMAX-2 coreference annotation tool[2], and the corpus was tokenized and split into sentences using the Europarl preprocessing tools[3]. Table 2 shows a breakdown of NP types of our markables for the three genres.

	Newswire	Stories	Med. leaflets
Named Entities	39.3	27.5	48.0
Personal pronouns	15.9	51.4	8.2
Definite NP	30.1	16.1	16.9
Relative pronouns	9.9	1.1	14.4
Indefinite NP	4.7	3.5	12.3
Other	0.1	0.4	0.2

Table 2: Types of NPs in the three genres (%)

3.3 Agreement

The English-German corpus was annotated by two lightly-trained independent annotators - students of linguistics. (For Russian, we had only one annotator available, therefore the agreement study will be done later.) For markables, we computed the inter-annotator agreement using Cohen's kappa in two settings: binary overlap and proportional overlap. For binary overlap, we consider two markables as "agreed" if they overlap by at least one token; proportional overlap measures the extent to which annotators agree on the identification of spans (number of overlapping tokens). For the coreference annotation, we computed MUC scores with strict mention matching. The results for the newswire texts and stories are shown in Table 3. For the medical leaflets, the results are somewhat lower: $\kappa = 0.76$ with binary overlap and 0.67 with proportional overlap; the MUC score is 70%. For the NP type attribute, Cohen's kappa for the texts from all genres on average is $\kappa = 0.94$.

	English	German
Binary overlap κ	0.87	0.86
Proportional overlap κ	0.81	0.81
MUC F-score	77.28	73.91

Table 3: Inter-annotator agreement for news and stories

4 Experiment

4.1 Experimental setup

Automatic sentence and word alignment. We aligned the source and target parts of the corpus at the sentence level using the HunAlign sentence aligner (Varga et al., 2007) and its wrapper LF Aligner[4], which already includes alignment dictionaries for the required language pairs.

Word alignment was performed with GIZA++ (Och and Ney, 2003) using the standard settings. Before the alignment, all texts in the corpus were tokenized and lower-cased using the Europarl preprocessing tools. The word aligner was trained on a collection of bilingual newswire text from our source given above, preprocessed in the same way as descibed above. The training set consists of around 200 000 parallel sentences for English-German, and 170 000 for English-Russian.

We computed both bidirectional alignments and the intersection of source-target / target-source alignments. (Annotation projection is often done with intersective alignments, as they provide higher precision than bidirectional alignments.) For English-German, we evaluated our word alignment against a set of 1000 manually annotated parallel sentences made available by S. Padó[5]. For English-Russian, we are not aware of any similar gold alignments and thus did not

[2]http://mmax2.sourceforge.net

[3]http://www.statmt.org/europarl/

[4]http://aligner.sourceforge.net

[5]http://nlpado.de/ sebastian/data/srl_data.shtml

evaluate. Results are given in Table 4. Following (Padó, 2007), we evaluated only the resulting intersective alignments. We compared our results to those of (Padó, 2007) and (Spreyer, 2011), who used the English-German part of the Europarl dataset. Our results are somewhat lower, probably due to the much smaller training set.

	Bisentences	Prec.	Recall	F-m.
Padó (2007)	1 029 400	98.6	52.9	68.86
Spreyer (2011)	1 314 944	94.88	62.04	75.02
Our alignment	205 208	92.95	51.23	66.05

Table 4: Evaluation of the automatic word alignment

To simplify subsequent processing, we converted the corpus annotations into the CoNLL table format[6] using discoursegraphs converter (Neumann, 2015).

Extraction of REs and transfer of coreference chains. For each RE in the source language we extract the corresponding RE in the target language, together with its coreference set number. Following the approach of Postolache et al. (2006), for each word span representing an RE in the source language, we extract the corresponding set of aligned words in the target language. The resulting target RE is the span between the first and the last extracted word, and it belongs to the same set as the source RE. Table 5 shows the number of REs and coreference chains projected through word alignment (from English).

4.2 Evaluation

We evaluate both the quality of the identification of mentions and the extraction of coreference chains using the CoNLL scorer[7].

1. Evaluation of the identification of mentions.

   We compute the scores for the identification of mentions using the strict mention matching as in the CoNLL-2011 (Pradhan et al., 2011) and CONLL-2012 shared tasks (Pradhan et al., 2012), so that we score only those projected markable spans that are exactly the same as the gold ones. The values for English-German and English-Russian are given in Table 6 as *mentions*.

2. Evaluation of coreference chains

[6]http://conll.cemantix.org/2012/data.html

[7]http://conll.cemantix.org/2012/software.html

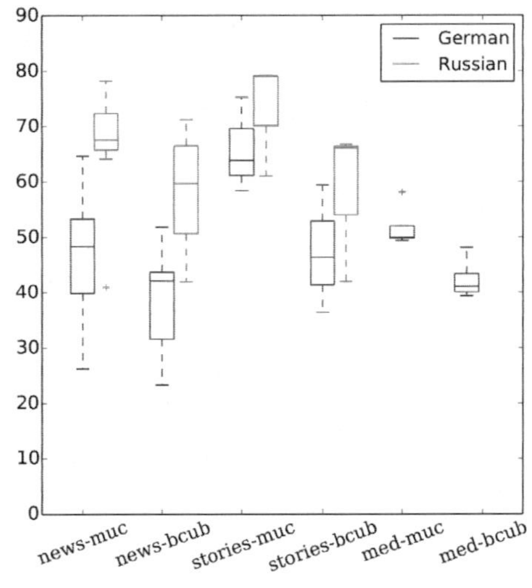

Figure 1: Comparison of English-German and English-Russian projections: boxplots of the macro-averaged F1 scores (MUC and B-cubed) for different genres

   We evaluate all the projected coreference chains against gold chains using the standard coreference evaluation metrics MUC (Vilain et al., 1995), CEAF (Luo, 2005) and B^3 (Bagga and Baldwin, 1998) to get complete performance characteristics. We also use strict matching as in the evaluation of the identification of mentions and evaluate the projected markables against all the markables of the gold standard. These scores depend on the identification of mentions evaluated in the previous step. We report the micro-averaged Precision, Recall and F-1 scores in Table 6. In addition, Figure 1 shows the distribution of macro-averaged F1-scores for two of the metrics (MUC and B^3) for both language pairs as boxplots.

3. Evaluation of coreference chains with minimal spans

   Finally, we evaluate using just minimal spans of the REs, i.e., syntactic heads. This indicates how well the REs can be projected, not punishing the algorithm for detecting only partially correct REs. We manually annotated syntactic heads of the gold and projected REs. Following the approach of Postolache et al. (2006), we select the leftmost

	Newswire		Stories		Medicine
	De	Ru	De	Ru	De
Transferred REs	465	493	329	357	214
Transferred coreference chains	122	122	44	44	82

Table 5: Number of REs and coreference chains transferred through bilingual projections

	Mentions			MUC			CEAF			B^3			Average (coref)		
	P	R	F1	P	R	F1	P	R	F1	P	R	F1	P	R	F1
de-News	61.5	48.6	54.3	55.9	43.2	48.7	58.6	46.7	51.9	45.8	34.2	39.1	53.4	41.4	46.6
de-Stories	82.0	54.5	65.5	81.9	51.6	63.3	81.7	53. 7	64.8	71.6	32.5	44.7	78.4	45.9	57.6
de-Medicine	61.2	44.7	51.7	66.2	42.7	51.9	59.1	43.3	50.0	53.43	35.16	42.41	59.6	40.4	48.1
de-$News_{min}$	89.9	71.2	79.4	87.3	66.2	75.3	85.5	67.5	75.5	80.4	58.1	67.5	84.4	63.9	72.8
de-$Stories_{min}$	95.4	62.2	75.3	94.4	58.5	72.2	95.1	61.2	74.5	90.9	40.2	55.7	93.5	53.3	67.5
de-$Medicine_{min}$	79.9	58.4	67.5	84.2	54.4	66.1	77.7	56.9	65.7	73.3	47.2	57.4	78.4	52.8	63.1
ru-News	79.3	64.5	71.2	76.3	60.7	67.6	76.3	62.0	68.4	69.0	52.2	59.4	73.9	58.3	65.1
ru-Stories	87.4	65.1	74.6	87.9	64.4	74.3	86.1	64.6	73.8	79.7	47.9	59.8	84.6	59.0	69.3
ru-$News_{min}$	90.9	72.6	80.7	89.6	69.8	78.5	87.3	69.7	77.5	83.7	61.4	70.9	86.9	67.0	75.6
ru-$Stories_{min}$	94.3	72.4	81.9	94.0	70.9	80.9	93.6	71.7	81.2	90.2	57.3	70.1	92.6	66.6	77.4

Table 6: Results for German and Russian: micro-averaged Precision, Recall, F1-score for different genres

noun, pronoun or numeral as head; otherwise, the RE is discarded. Results are given in Table 6 with the tag *'min'*.

4.3 Error Analysis

From a formal viewpoint, there are three categories of projection problems:

1. An RE is present in both source and target text, but it is not projected correctly, or not at all, on the grounds of mistakes in the word alignment phase.

2. An RE is present in the source text and correctly projected into the target text, but it does not show up in the gold standard, because the target language text does not have a corresponding RE *pair* (the target language does not reproduce the complete chain of the source).

3. An RE in the gold standard is not present in the target text and therefore can not be projected (the dual problem to (2): the source text does not have an RE pair that would correspond to one in the target text).

The number of errors caused by wrong word alignment (1) can be estimated on the basis of the alignment evaluation (Section 4.1), albeit only for the English-German language pair; due to the lack of resources, this is not possible for English-Russian.

Problems (2) and (3) are the more interesting ones for a qualitative error analysis. For this purpose, we visualized the projected files and the gold standard using the coreference module of the ICARUS corpus analysis platform (Gärtner et al., 2014). 50% of the data was randomly selected for the detailed analysis, and we determined the most frequent projection errors and categorized them into three different groups. Thereafter, we tried to verify our resulting hypotheses about variation in pronominal coreference in the three languages using a larger external corpus: InterCorp[8] (Čermák and Rosen, 2012) offers an online interface for searching parallel corpora in different languages and sub-corpora. We performed both monolingual and multilingual queries (e.g. querying one side of a parallel corpus vs. querying parallel data).

Further, we were interested in comparing our findings to available studies on multilingual nominal coreference in Contrastive Linguistics. However, the only work we found on this topic is a comparative study of nominal referring expressions for newswire texts in English and German (Kunz, 2010).

In our data, the problematic cases are those where the source language (SL) referring expression is missing or reformulated in the target text (TL), and therefore is not being projected. We identified three categories of errors caused by structural differences among the three languages:

[8] www.korpus.cz/intercorp.

Morphological differences.
These are cases of German contractions and compound nouns. For example, as in the case of *policy towards [minorities]*$_1$ and *[Minderheiten]politik*, the SL markable is not present in the TL as a separate unit, since we cannot split compound nouns and mark only a part. Also, cases like *zum Bahnhof* short for *zu dem Bahnhof* ('to the station') cause errors in the identification of spans, because we do not annotate prepositions as parts of markables on the English side. However, such cases are frequent in the German data, where, in general, the prepositions *an, bei, in, von, zu* can be contracted with subsequent determiners in written text. Our corpus study has shown that for the preposition *zu* ('to') the frequency of the contraction is 16 times higher than for the full form (InterCorp, measured in items per million (henceforth *i.p.m.*)).

Differences in NP syntax.
1: The use of articles. Some NPs are more frequently used with a definite article in German than in English, which resulted in the misidentification of spans. According to Kunz (2010), English allows the use of nouns with zero article more frequently than German. This is true for both singular and plural nouns. In our guidelines, nouns with zero article can only be linked to anaphoric pronouns (if any), but not between each other (like in OntoNotes). This resulted in mismatching chains: English NPs with zero article do not form chains and therefore cannot be projected, while the same NPs actually form a chain in German. For example:

(1) a. Lastly, the G-20 could also help drive momentum on *climate change*. <...> We also have to find a way to provide funding for adaptation and mitigation - to protect people from the impact of *climate change* and enable economies to grow while holding down pollution levels - while guarding against trade protection in the name of *climate change* mitigation.
b. Schließlich könnten die G-20 auch für neue Impulse im Bereich [des Klimawandels]$_1$ sorgen. Ebenso müssen wir einen Weg finden, finanzielle Mittel für die Anpassung an [den Klimawandel]$_1$ sowie dessen Eindämmung bereitzustellen - um die Menschen zu schützen und den Ökonomien Wachstum zu ermöglichen, aber den Grad der Umweltverschmutzung trotzdem in Grenzen zu halten. Außerdem gilt es, sich vor handelspolitischen Schutzmaßnahmen im Namen der Eindämmung [des Klimawandels]$_1$ zu hüten .

The query of InterCorp data has shown that German exhibits a higher number of NPs with definite article (57.928,55 i.p.m.) compared to English (31.405,22 i.p.m.). We also noticed that article use with named entities can vary in both languages (for example, the English *Hamas* corresponds to the German *die Hamas*). However, our corpus queries did not show any regularities yet; this issue requires a more detailed study regarding the types of named entities (which we assume to be the reason for the different use of articles). In the case of Russian, the absence of articles led to better results in the identification of REs, since in general, shorter spans increase the chance for a perfect alignment.

2: The use of reflexive pronouns. According to our annotation scheme, we annotated reflexive pronouns only when they are independent constituents (rather than verb particles), but we observe differences in the use of these pronouns for the three languages, so that in most cases these are non-parallel. These differences have to do with the form and distribution of reflexive pronouns. In English, we only have *-self* to express reflexivity, while in German and Russian a wider range of reflexives can be used. In German and Russian, it is possible to use more than one reflexive in a sentence to emphasize the action, which is not possible in English. As a result, there is less reflexives to be transferred from English to the target (German and Russian) sides of the corpus which led to errors in the projection.

3: Pre- and post-modification. In general, we noticed that German NPs allow more complicated premodification than English and Russian. According to Kunz (2010), English tends to postmodification, while German is less restrictive with premodification. These variations result in syntactical differences in markables and in non-parallelism.

Regarding the participial constructions, one of the complications is that in German, they occur only in pre-position, while in English and Russian they can be placed in both pre- and post-position. For example:

(2) a. Pakistan needs international help to bring hope to [*the young people*]$_1$ [*who*]$_1$ live there.
b. Pakistan braucht internationale Hilfe, um [*den dort lebenden jungen Menschen*]$_1$ Hoffnung zu bringen.

Non-equivalences in translation. The following cases of non-parallelism resulted in projection errors in our dataset; however, we could not find enough evidence to characterize them as systematic.

- Personal pronouns vs. indefinite pronouns.

  (3) a. $[It]_1$ was pursuing a two-pronged strategy.
  b. [*Man*] verfolgte eine Doppelstrategie. ('One followed a two-pronged strategy.')

  The German indefinite pronoun *man* is the target of the projected annotations, but it is not a markable according to our guidelines: it is non-referring and thus unable to participate in RE chains.

- Possessive NPs vs. adjectives. Some possessive NPs in the SL (for example, *the government of* $[India]_1$) can be expressed through adjectives in the TL (*die [indische] Regierung* or *indijskoe pravitel'stvo ([индийское] правительство)*) and therefore are no markables.

- Determiners vs. possessive pronouns. Personal pronouns in English can be translated as articles in German (for example, $[its]_1$ *broader goal = das weiter gefasste Ziel*), so that the source RE has no correspondent in the TL. For Russian, in this case a possessive form of a reflexive pronoun *svoj (свой)* can be used, or the possessive pronoun can be omitted.

- Relative clauses in one language can correspond to participle constructions or PPs in another. Examples:
  a. $[a\ fat\ lady]_1$ $[who]_1$ wore a fur around her neck
  b. $[eine\ dicke\ Dame\ mit\ einer\ Pelzstola]_1$ ('a fat lady with a a fur')

4.4 Comparing the genres

According to Table 6 and Figure 1, we see that newswire texts get the lowest scores, the reason most likely being the more complicated NPs. In setting 2 (evaluation of minimal spans), both newswire texts and stories obtain closer F1-scores, but the stories still have better precision scores. The medicine instruction leaflets in setting 2 have the worst results, and we observe lower improvement for precision between two settings compared to the newswire texts. This indicates that the quality of coreference resolution for medical texts depends to a higher degree on the coreference relations, than on the identification of mentions. In these texts, we frequently find borderline cases of non-/reference, when dieseases, parts of the body, etc. are being mentioned. Here, we will try to make the annotation guidelines more specific.

5 Discussion

The most closely related work is the approach of (Postolache et al., 2006), but some differences are noteworthy. In contrast to Postolache and colleagues, we do not focus on maximising precision; instead, our goal is to assess how well projection can work for all the annotations. In general, we use neither language-dependent software nor any additional linguistic information about the target language in the coreference projection and evaluation. Postolache et al., in contrast, applied a dedicated Romanian-English word aligner[9] (which achieves an F-score of 83.3% compared to our 66.05% of the language-independent GIZA++) and used special rules that rely upon the POS information and syntactic heads to produce their annotations, and then discarded the incorrectly projected ones (we used such rules only in the evaluation of the projected heads of REs). These rules reduced the number of gold and projected REs in the English-Romanian corpus considerably: from 3422 to 2491 (Postolache et al., 2006).

In our case, we use *all* REs to evaluate the spans of the projected annotations and the resulting coreference chains. Comparing our evaluation to Postolache's evaluation of all REs, we can see that our results yield a higher MUC precision for all of the genres (average 68.0 for English-German, 82.1 for English-Russian vs. 52.3 for English-Romanian), but a lower recall for both languages (45.8/62.6 vs. 82.04), which results in different F-measure (Postolache et al. obtained an average F1 of 63.9 compared to our F1 of 54.6 for German and 71.0 for Russian). This can be explained by the lower quality of our automatic English-German alignments compared to

[9]The COWAL word aligner is a lexical aligner which is adjusted only for Romanian-English and requires a corpus with morpho-syntactic annotations (Tufis et al., 2006).

the English-Romanian; the Russian REs were extracted slightly more accurately due to the structural differences in NPs. We also observed different scores for newswire texts, stories and medical leaflets, while Postolache et al. only used texts of one genre and in fact one author (different chapters of the same fiction book).

Keeping these different parameters in mind, in order to compare our results in a fair way, we evaluated the RE heads following the same rules to extract minimal spans of the projected REs, and evaluated them against manually annotated heads in the gold standard. In this setting, we obtained higher precision than in the previous setting, and in comparison to Postolache et al. (English-Romanian, avg. F1 = 80.5), our results are somewhat lower for English-German (avg. F1 = 74.1) and slightly better for English-Russian (avg. F1 = 81.3), which we attribute to the overall more difficult (and therefore more generalizable) projection scenario in our approach.

6 Conclusions

The goal of this study was to explore to what extent the coreference projection task can be tackled with a decidedly "light weight" approach. In contrast to earlier work, we used a well-known, standard word alignment tool trained on a corpus of moderate size. Furthermore, we deliberately worked with projecting English annotations to two relatively different languages, Russian and German, in order to study the limitations of the approach. In order to be as "generalizable" as possible (especially for other low-resourced languages), we work on the basis of common, relatively lean, annotation guidelines for coreference, which make few assumptions on the specifics of the languages considered here.

We compared our results quantitatively to the most closely related work and argued that they are competitive, in particular because our task setting is more target-language-neutral, we used three languages rather than two, and we worked on three different genres of text.

Our qualitative error analysis showed that problems are due to a set of structural differences of NPs in the three languages. Having completed this "light-weight" study, we will now move forward by introducing limited syntactic knowledge of the languages involved (NP chunking) and explore how much performance can be gained in that way. Still, our emphasis remains on devising procedures that are generalizable to other low-resourced languages, so we will do these extensions in small steps only.

Our annotation guidelines and other material will be made available via our website http://www.ling.uni-potsdam.de/acl-lab/.

References

Amit Bagga and Breck Baldwin. 1998. Algorithms for scoring coreference chains. In *The first international conference on language resources and evaluation workshop on linguistics coreference*, volume 1, pages 563–566.

František Čermák and Alexandr Rosen. 2012. The case of InterCorp, a multilingual parallel corpus. *International Journal of Corpus Linguistics*, 17(3):411–427.

Maud Ehrmann, Marco Turchi, and Ralf Steinberger. 2011. Building a multilingual named entity-annotated corpus using annotation projection. In *RANLP*, pages 118–124.

Markus Gärtner, Anders Björkelund, Gregor Thiele, Wolfgang Seeker, and Jonas Kuhn. 2014. Visualization, search, and error analysis for coreference annotations. In *Proceedings of 52nd Annual Meeting of the Association for Computational Linguistics: System Demonstrations*, pages 7–12.

Liane Guillou, Christian Hardmeier, Aaron Smith, Jörg Tiedemann, and Bonnie Webber. 2014. ParCor 1.0: A parallel pronoun-coreference corpus to support statistical MT. In *Ninth International Conference on Language Resources and Evaluation (LREC'14)*, pages 3191–3198. European Language Resources Association.

Sanda M. Harabagiu and Steven J. Maiorano. 2000. Multilingual coreference resolution. In *Proceedings of the sixth conference on Applied natural language processing*, pages 142–149. Association for Computational Linguistics.

Eduard Hovy, Mitchell Marcus, Martha Palmer, Lance Ramshaw, and Ralph Weischedel. 2006. OntoNotes: the 90% solution. In *Proceedings of the human language technology conference of the NAACL, Companion Volume: Short Papers*, pages 57–60. Association for Computational Linguistics.

Rebecca Hwa, Philip Resnik, Amy Weinberg, Clara Cabezas, and Okan Kolak. 2005. Bootstrapping parsers via syntactic projection across parallel texts. *Natural language engineering*, 11(03):311–325.

Olga Krasavina and Christian Chiarcos. 2007. PoCoS: Potsdam coreference scheme. In *Proceedings of the Linguistic Annotation Workshop*, pages 156–163. Association for Computational Linguistics.

Kerstin Anna Kunz. 2010. *Variation in English and German Nominal Coreference: A Study of Political Essays*, volume 21. Peter Lang.

Xiaoqiang Luo. 2005. On coreference resolution performance metrics. In *Proceedings of the conference on Human Language Technology and Empirical Methods in Natural Language Processing*, pages 25–32. Association for Computational Linguistics.

Rada Mihalcea, Carmen Banea, and Janyce M. Wiebe. 2007. Learning multilingual subjective language via cross-lingual projections. In *Proceedings of ACL-2007*.

Ruslan Mitkov and Catalina Barbu. 2002. Using bilingual corpora to improve pronoun resolution. *Languages in contrast*, 4(2):201–211.

Arne Neumann. 2015. discoursegraphs: A graph-based merging tool and converter for multilayer annotated corpora. In *Nordic Conference of Computational Linguistics NODALIDA 2015*, page 309.

Franz Josef Och and Hermann Ney. 2003. A systematic comparison of various statistical alignment models. *Computational linguistics*, 29(1):19–51.

Sylwia Ozdowska. 2006. Projecting POS tags and syntactic dependencies from English and French to Polish in aligned corpora. In *Proceedings of the International Workshop on Cross-Language Knowledge Induction*, pages 53–60. Association for Computational Linguistics.

Sebastian Padó and Mirella Lapata. 2005. Cross-linguistic projection of role-semantic information. In *Proceedings of the conference on Human Language Technology and Empirical Methods in Natural Language Processing*, pages 859–866. Association for Computational Linguistics.

Sebastian Padó. 2007. *Cross-lingual annotation projection models for role-semantic information*. Ph.D. thesis, German Research Center for Artificial Intelligence and Saarland University.

Oana Postolache, Dan Cristea, and Constantin Orasan. 2006. Transferring coreference chains through word alignment. In *Proceedings of LREC-2006*.

Sameer Pradhan, Lance Ramshaw, Mitchell Marcus, Martha Palmer, Ralph Weischedel, and Nianwen Xue. 2011. Conll-2011 shared task: Modeling unrestricted coreference in OntoNotes. In *Proceedings of the Fifteenth Conference on Computational Natural Language Learning: Shared Task*, pages 1–27. Association for Computational Linguistics.

Sameer Pradhan, Alessandro Moschitti, Nianwen Xue, Olga Uryupina, and Yuchen Zhang. 2012. CoNLL-2012 shared task: Modeling multilingual unrestricted coreference in OntoNotes. In *Joint Conference on EMNLP and CoNLL-Shared Task*, pages 1–40. Association for Computational Linguistics.

Altaf Rahman and Vincent Ng. 2012. Translation-based projection for multilingual coreference resolution. In *Proceedings of the 2012 Conference of the North American Chapter of the Association for Computational Linguistics: Human Language Technologies*, pages 720–730. Association for Computational Linguistics.

Asad Sayeed, Tamer Elsayed, Nikesh Garera, David Alexander, Tan Xu, Douglas W. Oard, David Yarowsky, and Christine Piatko. 2009. Arabic cross-document coreference detection. In *Proceedings of the ACL-IJCNLP 2009 Conference Short Papers*, pages 357–360. Association for Computational Linguistics.

Kathrin Spreyer. 2011. *Does it have to be trees?: Data-driven dependency parsing with incomplete and noisy training data*. Ph.D. thesis, Universitätsbibliothek Potsdam.

Jörg Tiedemann. 2009. News from OPUS-a collection of multilingual parallel corpora with tools and interfaces. In *Recent Advances in Natural Language Processing*, volume 5, pages 237–248.

Jörg Tiedemann. 2014. Rediscovering annotation projection for cross-lingual parser induction. In *Proc. COLING*.

Dan Tufis, Radu Ion, Alexandru Ceausu, and Dan Stefanescu. 2006. Improved lexical alignment by combining multiple reified alignments. In *EACL*.

Dániel Varga, Péter Halácsy, András Kornai, Viktor Nagy, László Németh, and Viktor Trón. 2007. Parallel corpora for medium density languages. *Amsterdam Studies in the Theory and History of Linguistics Science series 4*, 292:247.

Marc Vilain, John Burger, John Aberdeen, Dennis Connolly, and Lynette Hirschman. 1995. A model-theoretic coreference scoring scheme. In *Proceedings of the 6th conference on Message understanding*, pages 45–52. Association for Computational Linguistics.

David Yarowsky, Grace Ngai, and Richard Wicentowski. 2001. Inducing multilingual text analysis tools via robust projection across aligned corpora. In *Proceedings of the first international conference on Human language technology research*, pages 1–8. Association for Computational Linguistics.

Imed Zitouni and Radu Florian. 2008. Mention detection crossing the language barrier. In *Proceedings of the Conference on Empirical Methods in Natural Language Processing*, pages 600–609. Association for Computational Linguistics.

Projective methods for mining missing translations in DBpedia

Laurent Jakubina
RALI - DIRO
Université de Montréal
jakubinl@iro.umontreal.ca

Philippe Langlais
RALI - DIRO
Université de Montréal
felipe@iro.umontreal.ca

Abstract

Each entry (concept) in DBpedia comes along a set of surface strings (property rdfs:label) which are possible realizations of the concept being described. Currently, only a fifth of the English DBpedia entries have a surface string in French, which severely limits the deployment of Semantic Web Annotation for this language. In this paper, we investigate the task of identifying missing translations, contrasting two projective approaches. We show that the problem is actually challenging, and that a carefully engineered baseline is not easy to outperform.

1 Introduction

The LOD (Linked Open Data) (Bizer et al., 2009) is conceived as a language independent resource in the sense that the information is represented by abstract concepts to which "human-readable" strings — possibly in different languages — are attached, *e.g.* the rdfs:label property in DBpedia. For instance, we can access the abstract concept of computer by natural language queries such as ordinateur (rdfs:label@fr) in French or computer (rdfs:label@en) in English. Thanks to this, Semantic Web offers the advantage of having a truly multilingual World Wide Web (Gracia et al., 2012).

At the core of LOD, lies DBpedia (Jens Lehmann, 2014), the largest dataset that constitutes a hub to which most other LOD datasets are linked. [1] Since DBpedia is (automatically) generated from Wikipedia, which is multilingual, one would expect that each concept in DBpedia is labeled with a French surface string. This is for instance the case of the concept House of Commons of Canada[2] which is labeled in French as Chambre des communes du Canada. One problem, however, is that most labels are currently in English (Gómez-Pérez et al., 2013).

Indeed, the majority of datasets in LOD are primarily generated from the extraction of anglophone resources. DBpedia, the endogenous RDF dataset of Wikipedia is no exception here, since it proposes labels in French (rdfs:label@fr) for only one fifth[3] of the concepts. Of course, all concepts in English Wikipedia have at least one English label. For instance, the concept School life expectancy[4] has — at least at the time of writing — no label in French, while for instance, durée moyenne de scolarité appears in the (French) article Indice_de_développement_humain,[5] and is a good translation of the English term.

This situation comes from the fact that currently, a concept in DBpedia receives as its rdfs:label property in a given language the title of the Wikipedia article which is inter-language linked to the (English) Wikipedia article associated to the DBpedia concept.

The lack of surface strings in a foreign language does not only reduce the usefulness of RDF indexing engines such as sig.ma,[6] but also limits the deployment of Semantic Web Annotator (SWA) systems; *e.g.* (Mihalcea and Csomai, 2007; Milne and Witten, 2008). This motivates the present study, which aims at automatically mining French labels for the concepts in DBpedia that do not

[1] December 2014 - http://lod-cloud.net/

[2] http://dbpedia.org/page/House_of_Commons_of_Canada

[3] http://wiki.dbpedia.org/Datasets/DatasetStatistics

[4] http://dbpedia.org/page/School_life_expectancy

[5] http://fr.wikipedia.org/wiki/Indice_de_developpement_humain

[6] http://sig.ma

Long Paper Proceedings of the Eighth Workshop on Building and Using Comparable Corpora, pages 23–31,
Beijing, China, July 30, 2015.

possess one yet.

Identifying the translations of (English) Wikipedia article titles is partially solved in the BabelNet project (Navigli and Ponzetto, 2012). In this project, the translation of concepts in Wikipedia that are not inter-language linked are taken care of by applying machine translation on (minimum 3 and maximum 10) sentences extracted from Wikipedia that contain a link to the article whose title they seek to translate. The most frequent translation is finally selected. There are on the order of 500k articles in English Wikipedia that do not link to an article in French and which are not named entities (which typically do not require translation). BabelNet[7] provides a translation (not necessarily a good one) for 13% of them. This suggests that the projection of a resource such as `DBpedia` into French is not yet a solved problem.

In the remainder, we describe the approaches we tested in Section 2. Our experimental protocol is presented in Section 3. Section 4 reports the results we obtained. We conclude in Section 5.

2 Approaches

Identifying the translations of a term in a comparable corpus — two texts (one in each language of interest) that share similar topics without being in translation relation — is a challenge that has attracted many researchers. See (Sharoff et al., 2013) for a recent overview of the state-of-the-art in this field. In this work, we investigated several variants of two approaches for extracting translations from a comparable corpus: the seminal approach described in (Rapp, 1995) which uses a seed bilingual lexicon to induces new translations, and the approach of Bouamor et al. (2013) which instead exploits the Wikipedia structure. The latter approach has been shown to outperform the former significantly on a task of translating 110 terms in 4 different domains, making use of medium-sized corpora.[8]

2.1 Standard Approach (STAND)

The idea that the context of a term and the one of its translation share similarities that can be used to rank translation candidates has been previously investigated in (Rapp, 1995; Fung, 1998). Since then, many variants of this idea have been tested; see (Sharoff et al., 2013) for a recent discussion.

[7]Version 2.0.1 - March 2014

[8]400k words on the English side, 260k words on the French side.

	w_1	$\neg w_1$	
w_2	O_{11}	O_{12}	R_1
$\neg w_2$	O_{21}	O_{22}	R_2
	C_1	C_2	N

Table 1: Contingency table

We reproduced this approach in this work. In a nutshell, each term to be translated is represented by a so-called *context vector*; that is, the set of words that co-occur with this term in the source part of the corpus. An *association measure* is typically used to score the strength of the correlation between the term and the context words. Each translation candidate (typically each word of the target vocabulary) is similarly represented in the target language. Thanks to a *bilingual seed lexicon*, the source context vector is projected into a target one.[9] This projected target language vector is then compared to the vector of each of the target language candidates by the means of a *similarity measure*.

There are several parameters to the approach among which the size of the window used to collect co-occurrent words, the association and the similarity measures, as well as the seed lexicon.

We investigate the impact of the window size in section 4. We also compare two different association measures, namely the discontinuous odds-ratio (Evert, 2005, p. 86) named ORD hereafter, and the log-likelihood ratio (Dunning, 1993), named LLR, the most popular measures used in this line of work. Both measures (Eq. 1 and 2) are computed directly from the (monolingual) contingency table depicted in Table 1 for two words w_1 and w_2 where, for instance, O_{12} stands for the number of times w_1 occurs in a window, while w_2 does not.

$$\text{ORD}(w_1, w_2) = \log \frac{(O_{11} + \frac{1}{2})(O_{22} + \frac{1}{2})}{(O_{12} + \frac{1}{2})(O_{21} + \frac{1}{2})} \quad (1)$$

$$\text{LLR}(w_1, w_2) = 2 \sum_{ij} O_{ij} \log \frac{N \times O_{ij}}{R_i \times C_j} \quad (2)$$

[9]In our implementation, when no translation is found for a source word, the word is left as such in the target context vector. On the contrary, multiple translations are all added to the target context vector.

We did not investigate the impact of the nature and size of the bilingual seed lexicon, but decided to use one large lexicons comprising 116 354 word pairs populated from several available resources as well as an in-house bilingual lexicon.[10] A similar choice is made in (Bouamor et al., 2013) where a seed lexicon of approximately 120 000 entries is being used, and in (Hazem et al., 2013), where the the authors use a lexicon of 200 000 entries (before preprocessing).

Since in (Laroche and Langlais, 2010) the best performing variant uses the cosine similarity measure (Eq. 3), we used it in our experiments.[11]

$$cos(v_{src}, v_{trg}) = \frac{v_{src} \cdot v_{trg}}{\|v_{src}\| \cdot \|v_{trg}\|} \quad (3)$$

In the standard approach, the co-occurrent words are extracted from all the source documents of the comparable corpus in which the term to translate appears. We name this variant STAND hereafter.

2.2 Neighbourhood variants (LKI, LKO, CMP and RA)

Since we are interested in translating Wikipedia titles, a natural way of populating the context vector of a term is to consider the occurrences of this term in the article whose title we seek to translate. This avoids populating the context vector with words co-occurring with different senses of the word to translate. We implemented such a variant which is inherently facing the issue that too few occurrences of the term of interest may appear in a single article, especially in our case where the average length of a Wikipedia article is approximatively 1 400 words. Therefore we considered a variant which involves a *neighbourhood function*, that is, a function that returns a set of Wikipedia articles related to the one under consideration for translation. We investigated three such functions (as well as many combinations of them):

LKI(a) returns the set of articles that have a link pointing to the article a under consideration (in links). For instance, both `Computer_Science` and `Art` are two articles pointing to `Entertainment`.

LKO(a) returns the set of articles to which a points to (out links). For instance the article `Entertainment` points to `Party` and `Fun`.

CMP(a) returns the set of articles that are the most similar to a. We used the *MoreLikeThis* method of the search engine Lucene[12] for this. For instance, `Dance` and `Dance in Indonesia` are the top-2 documents returned by this function for the article `Entertainment`.

For sanity check purposes, we also considered the RND function which randomly returns articles. Note that the LKI() and LKO() functions were obtained with the Wikipedia Miner toolkit (Milne and Witten, 2013).

2.3 Explicit Semantic Analysis (ESA-B)

We also implemented the approach described in (Bouamor, 2014) which has been shown by the author to be more accurate than the aforementioned standard approach. The proposed method is an adaptation of the Explicit Semantic Analysis approach described in (Gabrilovich and Markovitch, 2007).

A term to translate is represented by the titles of the Wikipedia articles in which it appears. The projection of the resulting context vector into the target language is obtained by following the available inter-language links.[13] The words of the articles reached this way are candidates to the translation and are further ranked by a tf-idf schema. This approach avoids the need for a seed bilingual lexicon, but uses instead the structure of Wikipedia, and its multilingualism more particularly.

One meta-parameter of this approach is the maximum size of the context vector, that is, the maximum number of article titles to keep for describing a term. One might think that considering all the articles in which a term to translate is found is a good idea, but this strategy faces some sort of *semantic drift*. For instance, while translating the term `tears`, the context vector is populated with articles related to music albums that contain this term in their text content, while the associated French article (when available) almost never contains the translation. We investigate this meta-parameter in section 4. The other parameters were set as recommended in (Bouamor, 2014).

[10] Ergane (12 914 entries - `http://download.travlang.com`), Freelang (38 869 entries - `http://www.freelang.net`), as well as an in-house lexicon (99 747 entries).

[11] Actually, the authors reported that with the LLR association measure, the Dice similarity was a better choice, but we kept along with the cosine measure for simplicity.

[12] `http://www.lucene.org`

[13] Articles with no inter-language links are simply ignored.

3 Experimental Protocol

3.1 Comparable corpus

DBpedia is extracted from Wikipedia (Jens Lehmann, 2014). Thus, we downloaded the Wikipedia dump of June 2013 in both English and French. The English dump contains 4 262 946 articles, and the French one contains 1 398 932. Although some articles that share an inter-language link are parallel (Patry and Langlais, 2011), most article pairs are actually only comparable (Hovy et al., 2013).

3.2 English terms without translation

The vast majority (82,3%) of articles in the English Wikipedia do not have a link to an article in the French Wikipedia. We are interested to identify the translation of their title. Yet, we noticed that many of them are actually describing named entities (persons, geographic places, etc.), which typically do not require translation.[14] In order to filter named entities, we applied the BabelNet filter.[15] We ended up with a list of 521 895 (18,5%) terms we ultimately seek to translate. In this study, we further narrowed down our interest on unigrams.[16] This represents roughly 30% of those English terms.

3.3 Reference List

To evaluate our different approaches, we build a test set — a list of English source terms and their reference (French) translation. For this, we randomly sampled pairs of articles in Wikipedia that are inter-language linked. It is accepted that the titles of a pair of articles inter-language linked often constitute good translations (Hovy et al., 2013). Therefore, for each term (title) of our test set, we collected the associated title as a reference translation.

The sampling was done without considering named entities. For this purpose, we only considered article pairs which English title belongs to the bilingual lexicon we used as a seed lexicon for the STAND approach. Since the frequency of a source term is a key parameter of projective approaches, we also paid attention to vary the frequency range of the English terms we considered in our test set. More precisely, we gathered terms in those different ranges: infrequent [1-25], moderate [26-100], large [101-1000] and huge [1001+], where the frequency is the one in (English) Wikipedia. Some examples of pairs in each range are displayed in Table 2.

[1-25]	74 (8.5%)	
	myringotomy	paracentèse
[26-100]	267 (30.7%)	
	syllabification	césure
[101-1000]	259 (29.8%)	
	numerology	numérologie
[1001+]	269 (30.9%)	
	entertainment	divertissement
Total	869 (100%)	

Table 2: Distribution of the number of test forms at a given frequency range along with an example of an English term and its reference (French) translation.

We measured that using a large parallel corpus,[17] we could only identify the translation of roughly 1% of those terms, which indicates that parallel data might be of little interest in identifying the translations of Wikipedia article titles.

3.4 Evaluation

Our approaches have been configured to produce a ranked list of (at most) 20 candidates for each source (English) term. We compute two metrics to compare them: precision at rank 1 (P@1) which indicates the percentage of terms for which the best ranked candidate is the reference one, and Mean Average Precision at rank 20 (MAP-20), a measure commonly used in information retrieval (Manning et al., 2008) which averages precision at various recall rates.

3.5 Technical considerations

The standard approach (STAND) can be rather computation and time consuming, since any target word in Wikipedia is a potential candidate for

[14] Some languages do involve transliteration, but this is definitely beyond the scope of this paper.

[15] We used the `BabelSynset.getSynsetType()` function of the BabelNet API for this purpose.

[16] Methods that handle multi-word expressions typically embed single word translation (Morin and Daille, 2009); therefore our choice.

[17] We gathered 32 millions of sentence pairs from different available parallel corpora, including the GIGAWORD corpus we downloaded from `http://www.statmt.org/wmt13/translation-task.html`.

a given source term, and we are dealing with a rather large comparable corpus. Just as an illustration, the word `france` occurs more than 1 million times in the French Wikipedia, and its context vector potentially contains as much as 136 514 words (considering a context window of 6 words). Therefore, in our experiments, we only consider the first 50 000 occurrences of each term while populating the context vectors. Also, comparing source and target vectors can be time consuming, especially with context vectors of very high dimension. To save some time (and memory), we only represent a context vector (source or target) by (at most) the 1000 top-ranked terms according to the association measure being used.

4 Results

4.1 STAND

In some calibration experiments,[18] we observed that increasing the size of the window in which we collect the context words leads to noise (see Table 3). The optimal window size was 6 (3 words on each side of the word under consideration, excluding function words), which means that the cooccurrent words should be taken in the immediate vicinity of the term to translate. This corroborates the study in (Bullinaria and Levy, 2007). Therefore, we set the value of this meta-parameter to 6 in the remainder.

|window|	MAP-20
2	0.72
6	0.75
14	0.62
30	0.55

Table 3: MAP-20 of STAND (ORD) measured on a development set, as a function of the window size (counted in word).

The results of two variants of the standard approach are reported in Table 4 (line 1 and 2). Clearly, using ORD as an association measure drastically improves performance. This definitely corroborates the findings of Laroche and Langlais (2010). Still, the differences between both variants is surprisingly high: ORD delivers over six time higher performance than LLR does on average, while in the aforementioned work, the difference was much less marked.[19] Therefore, we use this association measure in the neighbourhood variants we tested.

We observed in practice the tendency of ORD to reward word pairs that appear often together even though the frequency of each word is very low. Thus, the context vector gathered with ORD tend to contain rare words that only appear in the context of the article under consideration. Those words offer a good discriminative power in our task, thus leading to much higher performance than the context vectors computed by LLR, which tend to gather more general related terms. This tendency can be observed in Figure 1 where ORD leads to a context vector with much more specific words. This observation deserves further investigations.

ORD	LLR
myringoplasty (16.32)	**tube** (147.6)
myringa (16.14)	**laser** (44.90)
laryngotracheal (15.13)	**procedure** (40.83)
tympanostomy (14.60)	usually (31.86)
laryngomalacia (14.19)	**knife** (30.13)
patency (13.43)	**myringoplasty** (29.85)
equalized (11.75)	**ear** (28.19)
grommet (11.58)	**laryngotracheal** (27.45)
obstructive (11.09)	**tympanostomy** (26.39)
incision (10.37)	cold (24.09)

Figure 1: Top words in the context vector computed with ORD and LLR for the source term `Myringotomy`. Words in bold appear in both context vectors.

A second observation that can be made is the strong correlation between the frequency of the term to translate and the performance of the approach. As a matter of fact, the performance for very frequent terms ([1001+]) is more than ten times the one measured on infrequent ones ([1–25]). This is a well-know fact that has been analyzed for instance in (Prochasson and Fung, 2011) where the authors report a precision of 60% for frequent test words (words seen at least 400 times), but only 5% for rare words (seen less than 15 times).

Overall, and even if a close comparison is difficult, the results we obtained for STAND are in-

[18] We used a development set of 125 (unigram) terms, considering a candidate list of 50k words randomly selected to which we added the reference translations.

[19] In Table 3 of their article, the authors measured on a test-set of 500 terms a MAP of 0.536 for ORD, and 0.413 for LLR.

	[1-25]		[26-100]		[101-1000]		[1001+]		[Total]	
	P@1	MAP	P@1	MAP	P@1	MAP	P@1	MAP	P@1	MAP
STAND (LLR)	0.000	0.003	0.011	0.019	0.019	0.023	0.134	0.154	0.051	0.061
STAND (ORD)	0.027	0.057	0.217	0.281	0.425	0.474	0.461	0.506	0.338	0.389
STAND (o-100)	0.027	0.058	0.146	0.201	0.154	0.219	0.104	0.162	0.125	0.182
LKI-1000	0.000	0.002	0.064	0.080	0.124	0.156	0.126	0.155	0.096	0.119
LKO-1000	0.000	0.000	0.016	0.022	0.089	0.119	0.033	0.046	0.044	0.058
CMP-1000	0.016	0.022	0.072	0.099	0.131	0.170	0.093	0.120	0.092	0.121
RND-1000	0.000	0.000	0.000	0.000	0.000	0.000	0.000	0.000	0.000	0.000
ESA-B	0.014	0.080	0.056	0.122	0.205	0.300	0.424	0.513	0.211	0.293

Table 4: Precision (at rank 1) and MAP-20 of some variants we tested. Each neighbourhood function was asked to return (at most) 1000 English articles. The ESA-B variant is making use of context vectors of (at most) 30 titles.

line with those reported in (Laroche and Langlais, 2010) that also focused on Wikipedia, but mining translations of medical terms. The authors reported a precision at rank one ranging from 20.7% up to 42.3% depending on test sets and configurations considered.

As we discussed in Section 3.5, due to computational issues, we cut the context vectors of the STAND approach after 1 000 terms. In order to measure how sensitive this cut-off is, we computed a variant where the top-100 terms only are kept (considering the association measure). The results of this variant are reported in line 3 of Table 4. As expected, the performance of the STAND approach drops significantly on average, and especially for very frequent terms ([1001+]).

4.2 Neighbourhood variants

We tested our neighbourhood functions as well as several combinations of them. One meta-parameter we investigated is the maximum number of articles returned by a function. We early observed that the more the better, something we explain shortly. Thereafter, each function was asked to return at most 1 000 articles. The results obtained by the 3 neighbourhood functions we described in section 2 are reported in lines 4 to 6 of Table 4.

Clearly, all the neighbourhood variants we considered yielded a significant drop in performance, which is disappointing from a practical point of view. This suggests that there is no obvious way to reduce the number of source documents to consider while populating the context vector of the term to translate. One explanation for this is that in our implementation, the context vector of each target candidate is computed by considering the full (French) Wikipedia collection. This dissymmetry introduces a mismatch between the source and target context vectors, leading to poor performances. A solution to this problem consists in computing target context vectors online from a subset of target documents of interest.[20] A drawback of this solution is (of course) that the computation must take place for each term to translate. This is left as a future work.

At least, the neighbourhood variants we experimented outperform the one where random documents are sampled (RND). This latter variant could not translate a single term of the test set.

4.3 ESA-B

In the default configuration of the approach described in (Bouamor et al., 2013), the authors limit the size of the context vector to 100, which we found suboptimal in our case. We varied the dimension of the context vectors and observed the best value to be 30 (see Table 5). This is the value used in the sequel.

|context|	MAP-20
10	0.248
20	0.287
30	0.293
50	0.291
100	0.271

Table 5: MAP-20 of ESA-B measured on the test set, as a function of the context vector dimension.

[20] This subset could, for instance, be defined by following the inter-language links of the source documents returned by the neighbourhood function.

Somehow contrary to what has been observed in (Bouamor et al., 2013), we observe that ESA-B (P@1 = 0.211) under-performs the STAND approach with the ORD association measure (P@1 = 0.338). One explanation for the difference is that, in (Bouamor et al., 2013), the authors filter in words such as nouns, verbs and adjectives when populating the context vectors, while we do not. This filter might interfere with the observation made in section 4.1 that, with ORD, rare words (which might be filtered out, such as URLs or even spelling mistakes) tend to appear in the context vectors, and happen to help in discriminating translations.

4.4 Analysis

If we consider the 528 test terms that appear over a hundred times in Wikipedia ([101+]), a test case where both approaches perform well, STAND (ORD) translates correctly 362 of them (considering the top-20 solutions), while ESA-B translates 351. If we had an oracle telling us which variant to trust for a given term, we could translate correctly 431 terms (81.6%), which indicates the complementarity of both approaches.

We analyzed the 97 terms for which our two approaches failed to propose the reference translation in the top-20 candidates and we identified a number of recurrent cases we describe hereafter.

First, English terms do appear in the French Wikipedia material that eventually get selected by the STAND approach. This is, for instance the case for the term `barber` (oracle translation: `coiffeur`) for which STAND proposed the translation `barber`.

Second, we observed that STAND (and perhaps ESA-B in a less systematic way) often proposes morphological variants of the reference translation. For instance, `coudre` (a verbal form) is the first proposed translation for `sewing`, while the reference translation is the noun `couture`.

Third, it happens in a few cases that the reference translation, although correct is very specific. Of course this penalizes equally both approaches we tested. For instance, the reference translation of `veneration` is `dulie`, while the first translation produced by STAND is `vénération` (a correct translation).

Also, and by far the most frequent case, we observed a *thesaurus effect* of both approaches where terms related to the source one are proposed. This effect can be observed in Figure 2 in which top candidates proposed by several variants we tested are reported for the terms exemplified in Table 2.

Finally, it happens that the top-20 candidates proposed are just noise (e.g. `noun` translated as `spora`).

5 Discussion

In this study, we implemented and compared two projective approaches for identifying the translation of terms that correspond to articles in English Wikipedia that do not have an inter-language link to an article in the French Wikipedia. Doing so would potentially help in enriching the `rdfs:label` property attached to concepts in `DBpedia`, thus easing semantic annotation in French. One method is a variant of the popular approach pioneered by (Rapp, 1995) which uses a bilingual seed lexicon for mapping source and target context vectors, and the other one has been proposed in (Bouamor et al., 2013) for which the authors shown to deliver state-of-the-art performance.

Among other things, our experiments suggest that the STAND approach performs as well or better than the ESA-B approach and combining both approaches, especially for high frequency terms might improve our results.

We also observed the well-known bias of those approaches toward frequent terms, which urges the need for methods adapted to less frequent terms. As a future work, we will investigate the solution proposed in (Prochasson and Fung, 2011) which is one step in this direction.

Also, the projective methods we considered embed several meta-parameters which values are sensible. It is therefore difficult to know a priori which configuration to chose for a given task, without conducting costly calibration experiments. Having at our disposal a number of different test cases would help in developing expertise in doing so. With the hope that this might help, the code and resources used in this work will be available at this url: `http://rali.iro.umontreal.ca/rali/?q=fr/Ressources`

Acknowledgments

This work has been funded by the Quebec funding agency *Fonds de Recherche Nature et Technologies* (FRQNT).

myringotomy [1-25]

ESA-B	–	laryngologie (0.209) oto (0.191) rhino (0.180) traitement (0.125) otite (0.080)
STAND (ORD)	–	permette (0.0489) devra (0.0473) scopie (0.0471) nécessitait (0.046) pût (0.045)
STAND (LLR)	–	melanosporum (0.274) neural (0.272) séminifère (0.269) ncathodique (0.269)

syllabification [26-100]

ESA-B	–	langues (0.517) consonne (0.420) langue (0.353) lettre (0.223) phonétique (0.166)
STAND (ORD)	–	modifier (0.079) suffit (0.074) vouloir (0.074) syllabique (0.074) intonation (0.072)
STAND (LLR)	–	édicté (0.106) exécutoire (0.097) syllabique (0.096) irrévocable (0.092)

numerology [101-1000]

ESA-B	20	œuvre (0.053) gematria (0.037) angels (0.031) nombres (0.029) chiffre (0.027)
STAND (ORD)	1	numérologie (0.095) occultisme (0.062) ésotérisme (0.062) divinatoire (0.058)
STAND (LLR)	5	jyotish (0.415) conditionaliste (0.412) karmique (0.364) domification (0.358)

entertainment [1001+]

ESA-B	2	entertainment (0.392) divertissement (0.151) vidéo (0.121) sony (0.111) jeu (0.073)
STAND (ORD)	–	beatmakers (0.012) manglobe (0.011) spycraft (0.011) déduplication (0.010)
STAND (LLR)	–	dsi (0.299) eshop (0.294) cocoto (0.231) ead (0.225) imagesoft (0.210)

Figure 2: Top candidates produced by several variants of interest for some test terms. The second column indicates the rank of the oracle translation when present in the top-20 returned list (or – if absent).

References

Christian Bizer, Tom Heath, and Tim Berners-Lee. 2009. Linked data-the story so far. *International journal on semantic web and information systems*, 5(3):1–22.

Dhouha Bouamor, Adrian Popescu, Nasredine Semmar, and Pierre Zweigenbaum. 2013. Building specialized bilingual lexicons using large scale background knowledge. In *EMNLP*, pages 479–489.

Dhouha Bouamor. 2014. *Constitution de ressources linguistiques multilingues à partir de corpus de textes parallèles et comparables*. PhD thesis, Université Paris Sud - Paris XI, February.

John A. Bullinaria and Joseph P. Levy. 2007. Extracting semantic representations from word cooccurrence statistics: A computational study. *Behavior Research Methods*, 39(3):510–526, August.

Ted Dunning. 1993. Accurate Methods for the Statistics of Surprise and Coincidence. *Comput. Linguist.*, 19(1):61–74, March.

Stefan Evert. 2005. *The statistics of word cooccurrences*. Ph.D. thesis, Dissertation, Stuttgart University.

Pascale Fung. 1998. A Statistical View on Bilingual Lexicon Extraction: From Parallel Corpora to Nonparallel Corpora. In *Proceedings of the Third Conference of the Association for Machine Translation in the Americas on Machine Translation and the Information Soup*, AMTA '98, pages 1–17, London, UK, UK. Springer-Verlag.

Evgeniy Gabrilovich and Shaul Markovitch. 2007. Computing semantic relatedness using wikipedia-based explicit semantic analysis. In *Proceedings of the 20th International Joint Conference on Artifical Intelligence*, IJCAI'07, pages 1606–1611, San Francisco, CA, USA. Morgan Kaufmann Publishers Inc.

Jorge Gracia, Elena Montiel-Ponsoda, Philipp Cimiano, Asunción Gómez-Pérez, Paul Buitelaar, and John McCrae. 2012. Challenges for the multilingual web of data. *Web Semantics: Science, Services and Agents on the World Wide Web*, 11:63–71, March.

Asunción Gómez-Pérez, Daniel Vila-Suero, Elena Montiel-Ponsoda, Jorge Gracia, and Guadalupe Aguado-de Cea. 2013. Guidelines for multilingual linked data. In *Proceedings of the 3rd International Conference on Web Intelligence, Mining and Semantics*, WIMS '13, pages 3:1–3:12, New York, NY, USA. ACM.

Amir Hazem, Morin Emmanuel, and others. 2013.

Word co-occurrence counts prediction for bilingual terminology extraction from comparable corpora. *IJCNLP 2013.*

Eduard Hovy, Roberto Navigli, and Simone Paolo Ponzetto. 2013. Collaboratively built semi-structured content and artificial intelligence: The story so far. *Artificial Intelligence*, 194:2–27, January.

Robert Isele Jens Lehmann. 2014. DBpedia - a large-scale, multilingual knowledge base extracted from wikipedia. *Semantic Web Journal.*

Audrey Laroche and Philippe Langlais. 2010. Revisiting context-based projection methods for term-translation spotting in comparable corpora. In *Proceedings of the 23rd International Conference on Computational Linguistics*, COLING '10, pages 617–625, Stroudsburg, PA, USA. Association for Computational Linguistics.

Christopher D. Manning, Prabhakar Raghavan, and Hinrich Schütze. 2008. *Introduction to Information Retrieval.* Cambridge University Press, New York, NY, USA.

Rada Mihalcea and Andras Csomai. 2007. Wikify!: linking documents to encyclopedic knowledge. In *Proceedings of the sixteenth ACM conference on Conference on information and knowledge management*, pages 233–242. ACM.

David Milne and Ian H. Witten. 2008. Learning to link with wikipedia. In *Proceedings of the 17th ACM conference on Information and knowledge management*, pages 509–518. ACM.

David Milne and Ian H. Witten. 2013. An open-source toolkit for mining wikipedia. *Artif. Intell.*, 194:222–239, January.

Emmanuel Morin and Béatrice Daille. 2009. Compositionality and lexical alignment of multi-word terms. *Language Resources and Evaluation*, page 0, August.

Roberto Navigli and Simone Paolo Ponzetto. 2012. BabelNet: The automatic construction, evaluation and application of a wide-coverage multilingual semantic network. *Artificial Intelligence*, 193:217–250, December.

Alexandre Patry and Philippe Langlais. 2011. Identifying Parallel Documents from a Large Bilingual Collection of Texts: Application to Parallel Article Extraction in Wikipedia. In *Proceedings of the 4th Workshop on Building and Using Comparable Corpora: Comparable Corpora and the Web*, BUCC '11, pages 87–95, Stroudsburg, PA, USA. Association for Computational Linguistics.

Emmanuel Prochasson and Pascale Fung. 2011. Rare word translation extraction from aligned comparable documents. In *Proceedings of the 49th Annual Meeting of the Association for Computational Linguistics: Human Language Technologies - Volume 1*, HLT '11, pages 1327–1335, Stroudsburg, PA, USA. Association for Computational Linguistics.

Reinhard Rapp. 1995. Identifying word translations in non-parallel texts. In *Proceedings of the 33rd Annual Meeting on Association for Computational Linguistics*, ACL '95, pages 320–322, Stroudsburg, PA, USA. Association for Computational Linguistics.

Serge Sharoff, Reinhard Rapp, and Pierre Zweigenbaum. 2013. Overviewing important aspects of the last twenty years of research in comparable corpora. In Serge Sharoff, Reinhard Rapp, Pierre Zweigenbaum, and Pascale Fung, editors, *Building and Using Comparable Corpora*, pages 1–17. Springer Berlin Heidelberg.

Attempting to Bypass Alignment from Comparable Corpora via Pivot Language

Alexis Linard **Béatrice Daille** **Emmanuel Morin**
Université de Nantes, LINA UMR CNRS 6241
2 rue de la Houssinière, BP 92208
44322 Nantes Cedex 03, France
firstname.lastname@univ-nantes.fr

Abstract

Alignment from comparable corpora usually involves two languages, one source and one target language. Previous works on bilingual lexicon extraction from parallel corpora demonstrated that more than two languages can be useful to improve the alignments. Our works have investigated to which extent a third language could be interesting to bypass the original alignment. We have defined two original alignment approaches involving pivot languages and we have evaluated over four languages and two pivot languages in particular. The experiments have shown that in some cases the quality of the extracted lexicon has been enhanced.

1 Introduction

The main goal of this work is to investigate to which extent bilingual lexicon extraction using comparable corpora can be improved using a third language when dealing with poor resource language pairs. Indeed, the quality of the result of the extracted bilingual lexicon strongly depends on the quality of the resources, that is to say the corpora and a general language bilingual dictionary. In this study, we stress the key role of the potential high quality resources of the pivot language (Chiao and Zweigenbaum, 2004; Morin and Prochasson, 2011; Hazem and Morin, 2012). The idea of involving a third language is to benefit from the lexical information conveyed by the additional language. We also assume that in the case of not so usual language pairs the two comparable corpora are of medium quality, and the bilingual dictionary seems weak, due to the nonexistence of such a dictionary. We expect as a consequence a bad quality of the extracted lexicon. Nevertheless, we are highly confident that a language for which we have of a lot of resources can thwart the effect of the poor original resources. English is probably the first language in term of work and resources in Natural Language Processing, hence it can appear as a good candidate as pivot language.

The paper is organized as follows: we give a short overview of bilingual lexicon extraction standard method in Section 2. Our proposed approaches are described in Section 3. The resources we have used are presented in Section 4 and experimental results in Section 5. Finally, we expose further works and improvements in Sections 6 and 7.

2 Bilingual Lexicon Extraction

Initially designed for parallel corpora (Chen, 1993), and due to the scarcity of this kind of resources (Martin et al., 2005), bilingual lexicon extraction then tried to deal with comparable corpora instead (Fung, 1995; Rapp, 1995). An algorithm using comparable corpora is the standard method (Fung and McKeown, 1997) closely based on the notion of context vectors. Many implementations have been designed in order to do so (Rapp, 1999; Chiao and Zweigenbaum, 2002; Morin et al., 2010). A context vector $\mathbf{w}$ is, for a given word w, the representation of its contexts $ct_1 \ldots ct_i$ and the number of occurrences found in the window of a corpus. In this approach, context vectors are calculated both in source and target languages corpora. They are also normalized according to association scores. Then, thanks to a seed dictionary, source context vectors are transferred into target language. The similarity between the translated context vector $\overline{\mathbf{w}}$ for a given source word w to translate and all target context vectors $\mathbf{t}$ lead to the creation of a list of ranked candidate translations. The rank is function of the similarity between context vectors so that the closer they are, the better the ranked translation is.

Research in this field aims at improving the

Short Paper Proceedings of the Eighth Workshop on Building and Using Comparable Corpora, pages 32–37,
Beijing, China, July 30, 2015. ©2015 Association for Computational Linguistics

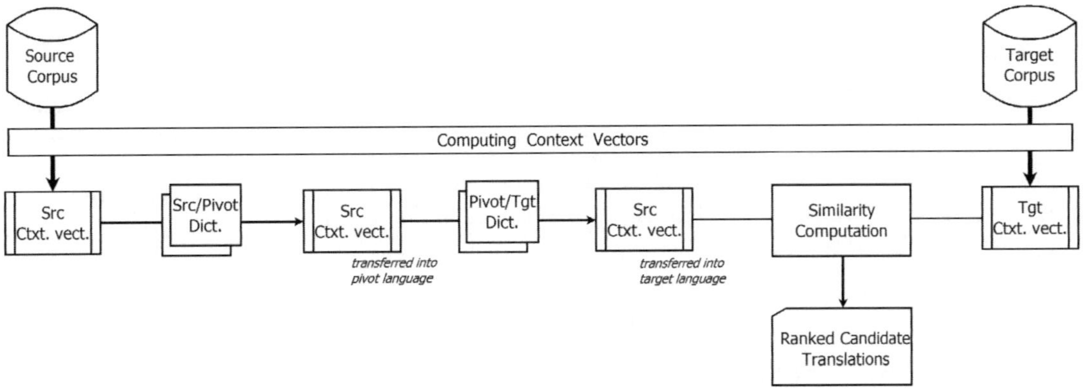

Figure 1: Transferring Context Vectors Successively.

quality of the extracted lexicon. For instance, we can cite the use of a bilingual thesaurus (Déjean et al., 2002), implication of predictive methods for word co-occurrence counts (Hazem and Morin, 2013) or the use of unbalanced corpora (Morin and Hazem, 2014). Among them, and in the case of comparable corpora, we can denote that none looked into pivot-language approaches.

Nevertheless, the idea of involving a pivot language for translation tasks is not recent. Bilingual lexicon extraction from parallel corpora has already been improved via the use of an intermediary language (Kwon et al., 2013; Seo et al., 2014; Kim et al., 2015), so does statistical translation (Simard, 1999; Och and Ney, 2001). Those works lay on the assumption that another language brings additional information (Dagan and Itai, 1991).

3 Alignment Approaches with Pivot Language

In this paper, we present two original approaches which derive from the standard method and involve a third language. We assume that the bilingual dictionary is unavailable or of low quality, but that the source/pivot and pivot/target dictionaries are much better.

3.1 Transferring Context Vectors Successively

The first method, and the most naive is to translate context vectors successively, to start with from source to pivot language, and to follow from pivot to target language. Hence, the context vectors in the source language are computed as it is usually done in the standard method. Then, the second step is to transfer them into the pivot language thanks to a source/pivot dictionary. This operation is done a second time from pivot to target language with a pivot/target dictionary in order to obtain source context vectors translated into target language. We can say that we transferred the context vectors *via* a pivot language. Finally, the last step of similarity computation stays unchanged: for one source word w for which we want to find the translation in target language, we compute the similarity between its context vector transferred successively $\overline{\overline{\mathbf{w}}}$ and all target context vectors $\mathbf{t}$. This method is presented in Figure 1.

3.2 Transposing Context Vectors to Pivot Language

The second method based on pivot dictionaries consists in translating both source and target context vectors into pivot language. Thus, the operation of computing similarity occurs in the vectorial space of the pivot language. In order to do so, the context vector of a word in source language to translate is computed as it is usually done in the standard method. The second step is to transfer the source and target context vectors into the pivot language using source/pivot and target/pivot dictionaries. At this stage, we gather in the pivot language the translated source and all target context vectors. The next and last operation is to compute the similarity between the source context vector transferred into pivot language $\overline{\mathbf{w}}$ and all target context vectors transferred into pivot language $\overline{\mathbf{t}}$. This method is presented in Figure 2.

4 Multilingual Resources

In this paper, we perform translation-candidate extraction from all pairs of languages from/to En-

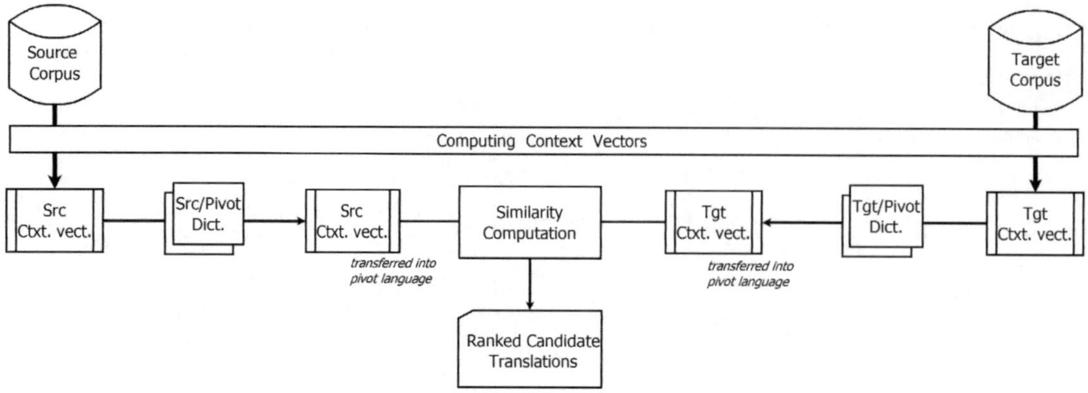

Figure 2: Transposing Context Vectors to Pivot Language.

glish, French, German and Spanish and involving English or French as the pivot language. The use of those pivot languages in particular is motivated by two factors: first, English, because it is the language *by default* we have of in a quasi infinite amount of data, and last, French, because we know that our resources (corpus and dictionaries) are of good quality.

4.1 Comparable Corpora

The first comparable corpus we used during our experiments is the *Wind Energy corpus*[1]. It was built from a crawl of webpages using many keywords related to the wind energy field. The comparable corpus is composed of documents in 7 languages, among others German, English, Spanish and French. The second comparable corpus we used is the *Mobile Technologies corpus*. It was also built by crawling the web. Both of them were composed of 300k to 470k words in each language.

4.2 Bilingual Dictionaries

	EN-DE DE-EN	EN-ES ES-EN	EN-FR FR-EN	FR-ES ES-FR	FR-DE DE-FR	DE-ES ES-DE
#entr.	600k	26k	240k	100k	170k	15k

Table 1: Number of entries in each dictionary.

In order to perform bilingual lexicon extraction from comparable corpora, a bilingual dictionary was mandatory. Nevertheless, we only have of French/English, French/Spanish and French/German dictionaries from the ELRA catalogue[2]. These dictionaries were generalist, and contained few terms related to the Wind Energy and Mobile Technologies domains. So, the French/English, French/Spanish and French/German were reversed to obtain English/French, Spanish/French and German/French dictionaries. As for the others, they were built by triangulation from the ones above (see Table 1). As a consequence, we expect those dictionaries to be very mediocre.

4.3 Reference Lists

	EN	FR	ES	DE
WE	48	58	55	55
MT	52	58	60	88

Table 2: Number of SWT in reference lists.

In order to evaluate the output of the different approaches, terminology reference lists were built from each corpus in each language (Loginova et al., 2012). Depending on the corpus and the language, the lists were composed of 48 to 88 single word terms (abbreviated SWT – see Table 2).

5 Experiments and Results

Pre-processing French, English, Spanish and German documents were pre-processed using TTC TermSuite (Rocheteau and Daille, 2011)[3]. The operations done during pre-processing were the following: tokenization, part-of-speech tagging and lemmatization. Moreover, function words and hapaxes had been removed.

[1] http://www.lina.univ-nantes.fr/?Ressources-linguistiques-du-projet.html

[2] http://catalog.elra.info/

[3] https://logiciels.lina.univ-nantes.fr/redmine/projects

		Wind Energy					Mobile Technologies				
Lang.	Pivot	Std.	P_1	P_2	R_{MAX}	C	Std.	P_1	P_2	R_{MAX}	C
EN-ES	FR	0.268	**0.390**	**0.374**	*0.646*	65.76%	0.445	**0.523**	**0.467**	*0.882*	66.52%
ES-EN	FR	0.119	**0.232**	**0.233**	*0.491*		0.193	**0.272**	**0.321**	*0.533*	
EN-DE	FR	0.158	0.125	**0.215**	*0.458*	66.21%	0.622	0.205	0.570	*0.896*	68.95%
DE-EN	FR	0.018	0.018	0.018	*0.200*		0.074	0.070	0.069	*0.455*	
FR-DE	EN	0.056	**0.118**	**0.132**	*0.418*	77.63%	0.053	**0.063**	**0.061**	*0.597*	80.06%
DE-FR	EN	0.038	0.028	0.028	*0.151*		0.034	0.023	0.026	*0.432*	
FR-ES	EN	0.366	0.150	0.176	*0.528*	82.36%	0.514	0.275	0.280	*0.807*	82.02%
ES-FR	EN	0.210	0.103	0.117	*0.357*		0.238	0.207	0.186	*0.552*	
ES-DE	FR	0.000	**0.041**	**0.097**	*0.273*	44.24%	0.001	**0.058**	**0.067**	*0.500*	44.02%
	EN	0.000	**0.045**	**0.027**			0.001	**0.033**	**0.035**		
DE-ES	FR	0.001	**0.018**	**0.018**	*0.218*		0.126	**0.355**	**0.347**	*0.585*	
	EN	0.001	**0.018**	**0.018**			0.126	**0.189**	**0.179**		

Table 3: MRR achieved for pivot dictionary based approaches.

Context vectors In order to compute and normalize context vectors, the value $a(ct)$ associated to each co-occurrence ct of a given word w in the corpus was computed. Such value could be computed thanks to Log Likelihood (Fano and Hawkins, 1961) or Mutual Information (Dunning, 1993) for instance. Among them we chose Log Likelihood as its representativity is the most accurate (Bordag, 2008). Context vectors were computed by TermSuite, as one of its components performed this operation.

Similarity measures The so-called similarity could be computed according to Cosine similarity (Salton and Lesk, 1968) or Weighted Jaccard Distance (Grefenstette, 1994). We decided to only present the results achieved using Cosine similarity. The differences between them in term of Mean Reciprocal Rank (MRR) were insignificant.

$$\text{Cosine}\,(\overline{\mathbf{w}}, \mathbf{t}) = \frac{\sum_k a(\overline{\mathbf{w}}_k)a(\mathbf{t_k})}{\sqrt{\sum_k a(\overline{\mathbf{w}}_k)^2}\sqrt{\sum_k a(\mathbf{t_k})^2}}$$

Evaluation metrics In order to evaluate our approaches, we used Mean Reciprocal Rank (Voorhees, 1999). The strength of this metric is that it takes into account the rank of the candidate translations. Hereinafter, the MRR defined as follows (t stands for the terms to evaluate and r_t for the rank achieved by the system for the good translation of t):

$$MRR = \frac{1}{|t|} \times \sum_{k=1}^{|t|} \left(\frac{1}{r_{t_k}}\right)$$

Results The MRR achieved for both approaches is shown in Table 3 for Wind Energy and Mobile Technologies corpora respectively. We present, for the sake of comparison, the results achieved by the standard method (Std.), method transferring context vectors successively (P_1) and the method transposing context vectors to pivot language (P_2). We also give additional information, such as the best achievable result according to the reference lists and the words belonging to the filtered corpus (R_{MAX}) and corpora comparability C (Li and Gaussier, 2010).

The corpus comparability metric consists in the expectation of finding the translation in target language for each source word in the corpus. Therewith, it is a good way of measuring the distributional symmetry between two corpora and given a dictionary. We can also notice that the Maximun Recall R_{MAX} is quite low for some pairs of languages: this is due to the high number of hapaxes belonging to the reference lists that were filtered out during pre-processing.

According to the results, we can see that there is a strong correlation between the improvements achieved by pivot based approaches and corpus comparability. We have improved the quality of the extracted bilingual lexicon only in the case of poorly comparable corpora, respectively $\leq 65.76\%$ and $\leq 66.52\%$ for Wind Energy and Mobile Technologies corpora. For instance, we have increased the MRR from 0.268 to 0.390 and 0.374 in the case of translation from English to Spanish for the Wind Energy corpus, and from 0.126 to 0.355 and 0.347 for German to Spanish via French for the Mobile Technologies corpus.

6 Discussion

In Section 5 we have shown up that results can be enhanced only in the case of poorly comparable pairs of languages. For fairly comparable corpora

	EN-DE DE-EN	EN-ES ES-EN	EN-FR FR-EN	FR-ES ES-FR	FR-DE DE-FR	DE-ES ES-DE
WE	66.21%	65.76%	80.23%	82.36%	77.63%	44.24%
MT	68.95%	66.52%	80.99%	82.02%	80.06%	44.02%

Table 4: Corpora comparability.

($\leq 68\% \leq C \leq 80\%$), results remain unchanged in comparison with the standard approach. Finally, for highly comparable corpora ($C > 80\%$) the quality of the extracted lexicon gets worse.

The interpretation we suggest is the following: given two corpora, S in source language, T in target and a bilingual dictionary source/target $\mathcal{D}$, the comparability is function of S, T, $\mathcal{D}_{S/T}$. Therefore, a low comparability measure can be due to a poor expectation of finding the translation in target language for each source word in the corpus because the two corpora are not lexically close enough, or because the dictionary is weak. We checked this second option, and this is how we substantiate the pivot dictionary based approaches. Thus, the use of source/pivot $\mathcal{D}_{S/P}$ and pivot/target $\mathcal{D}_{P/T}$ dictionary can artificially improve the comparability and enhance the extracted lexicon. We have also remarked that the coverage of dictionaries is an important factor: a large dictionary is better than a shorter.

Of course, we do not pretend that our methods can compare with an initially very highly comparable corpora since the use of pivot dictionaries will introduce more noise than it will bring additional information.

7 Conclusion

We have presented two pivot based approaches for bilingual lexicon extraction from comparable specialized corpora. Both of them lay on pivot dictionaries. We have shown that the bilingual lexicon extraction depends on the quality of the resources. Furthermore, we have also demonstrated that the problem can be fixed involving a third strongly supported language such as English for instance. We have also carried out that the enhancements are function of the comparability of the corpora. These first experiments have shown that using a pivot language can make improvements in the case of poorly comparable initial corpora.

In future works, we will try to benefit from the information brought by an unbalanced pivot corpus. Unlike this article in which we have only looked into pivot dictionaries in order to increase the comparability of the source and target corpora, we think that the next step is to reshape context vectors with a pivot corpus. In addition, we will see whether linear regression models to reshape context vectors can make improvements or not.

Acknowledgments

This work is supported by the French National Research Agency under grant ANR-12-CORD-0020.

References

Stefan Bordag. 2008. A comparison of co-occurrence and similarity measures as simulations of context. In *Proceedings of the 9th International Conference on Computational Linguistics and Intelligent Text Processing*, pages 52–63. Haifa, Israel.

Stanley F. Chen. 1993. Aligning sentences in bilingual corpora using lexical information. In *Proceedings of the 31st Annual Meeting on Association for Computational Linguistics*, pages 9–16, Columbus, Ohio, USA.

Yun-Chuang Chiao and Pierre Zweigenbaum. 2002. Looking for candidate translational equivalents in specialized, comparable corpora. In *Proceedings of the 19th International Conference on Computational Linguistics*, pages 1–5, Taipei, Taiwan.

Yun-Chuang Chiao and Pierre Zweigenbaum. 2004. Aligning words in french-english non-parallel medical texts: Effect of term frequency distributions. In *Medinfo 2004: Proceedings of the 11th World Congress on Medical Informatics*, pages 23–27, Amsterdam, Netherlands. Ios Pr Inc.

Ido Dagan and Alon Itai. 1991. Two languages are more informative than one. In *Proceedings of the 29th Annual Meeting of the Association for Computational Linguistics*, pages 130–137, Berkeley, California, USA.

Hervé Déjean, Éric Gaussier, and Fatia Sadat. 2002. An approach based on multilingual thesauri and model combination for bilingual lexicon extraction. In *Proceedings of the 19th international conference on Computational linguistics*, pages 1–7, Taipei, Taiwan.

Ted Dunning. 1993. Accurate methods for the statistics of surprise and coincidence. *Computational linguistics*, 19(1):61–74.

Robert M Fano and David Hawkins. 1961. Transmission of information: A statistical theory of communications. *American Journal of Physics*, 29(11):793–794.

Pascale Fung and Kathleen McKeown. 1997. Finding terminology translations from non-parallel corpora. In *Proceedings of the 5th Annual Workshop on Very Large Corpora*, pages 192–202, Beijing, China.

Pascale Fung. 1995. Compiling bilingual lexicon entries from a non-parallel english-chinese corpus. In *Proceedings of the 3rd Annual Workshop on Very Large Corpora*, pages 173–183, Cambridge, Massachusetts, USA.

Gregory Grefenstette. 1994. *Explorations in automatic thesaurus discovery*. Springer Science & Business Media.

Amir Hazem and Emmanuel Morin. 2012. Adaptive Dictionary for Bilingual Lexicon Extraction from Comparable Corpora. In *Proceedings of the 8th international conference on Language Resources and Evaluation (LREC)*, pages 288–292, Istanbul, Turkey.

Amir Hazem and Emmanuel Morin. 2013. Word Co-occurrence Counts Prediction for Bilingual Terminology Extraction from Comparable Corpora. In *6th International Joint Conference on Natural Language Processing.*, pages 1392–1400, Nagoya, Japan.

Jae-Hoon Kim, Hong-Seok Kwon, and Hyeong-Won Seo. 2015. Evaluating a pivot-based approach for bilingual lexicon extraction. *Computational Intelligence and Neuroscience*, 2015.

Hong-seok Kwon, Hyeong-won Seo, and Jae-hoon Kim. 2013. Bilingual lexicon extraction via pivot language and word alignment tool. In *Proceedings of the Sixth Workshop on Building and Using Comparable Corpora*, pages 11–15, Sofia, Bulgaria, August.

Bo Li and Eric Gaussier. 2010. Improving corpus comparability for bilingual lexicon extraction from comparable corpora. In *Proceedings of the 23rd International Conference on Computational Linguistics*, pages 644–652, Beijing, China.

Elizaveta Loginova, Anita Gojun, Helena Blancafort, Marie Guégan, Tatiana Gornostay, and Ulrich Heid. 2012. Reference lists for the evaluation of term extraction tools. In *Proceedings of the 10th International Congress on Terminology and Knowledge Engineering*, Madrid, Spain.

Joel Martin, R Mihalcca, and Ted Pedersen. 2005. Word alignment for languages with scarce resources. In *Proceedings of The ACL Workshop on Building and Using Parallel Text*, pages 65–74, Ann Arbor, Michigan, USA.

Emmanuel Morin and Amir Hazem. 2014. Looking at Unbalanced Specialized Comparable Corpora for Bilingual Lexicon Extraction. In *Proceedings of the 52nd Annual Meeting of the Association for Computational Linguistics*, pages 1284–1293, Baltimore, USA.

Emmanuel Morin and Emmanuel Prochasson. 2011. Bilingual lexicon extraction from comparable corpora enhanced with parallel corpora. In *Proceedings of the 4th Workshop on Building and Using Comparable Corpora*, pages 27–34, Portland, Oregon, USA.

Emmanuel Morin, Béatrice Daille, Kyo Kageura, and Koichi Takeuchi. 2010. Brains, not Brawn: The Use of "Smart" Comparable Corpora in Bilingual Terminology Mining. *ACM Transactions on Speech and Language Processing (TSLP)*, 7(1):1–23.

Franz Josef Och and Hermann Ney. 2001. Statistical multi-source translation. In *Machine Translation Summit*, pages 253–258, Santiago de Compostela, Spain.

Reinhard Rapp. 1995. Identifying word translations in non-parallel texts. In *Proceedings of the 33rd Annual Meeting on Association for Computational Linguistics*, pages 320–322, Cambridge, Massachusetts, USA.

Reinhard Rapp. 1999. Automatic identification of word translations from unrelated english and german corpora. In *Proceedings of the 37th Annual Meeting of the Association for Computational Linguistics on Computational Linguistics*, pages 519–526.

Jérôme Rocheteau and Béatrice Daille. 2011. TTC TermSuite: A UIMA Application for Multilingual Terminology Extraction from Comparable Corpora. In *Proceedings of the 5th International Joint Conference on Natural Language Processing*, pages 9–12, Chiang Mai, Thailand.

Gerard Salton and Michael E Lesk. 1968. Computer evaluation of indexing and text processing. *Journal of the ACM*, 15(1):8–36.

Hyeong-Won Seo, Hong-Seok Kwon, and Jae-Hoon Kim. 2014. Extended pivot-based approach for bilingual lexicon extraction. *Journal of the Korean Society of Marine Engineering*, 38(5):557–565.

Michel Simard. 1999. Text-translation alignment: Three languages are better than two. In *Proceedings of Empirical Methods in Natural Language Processing and Very Large Corpora*, pages 2–11, College Park, Maryland, USA.

Ellen M. Voorhees. 1999. The trec-8 question answering track report. In *Proceedings of TREC-8*, volume 99, pages 77–82.

Application of a Corpus to Identify Gaps between English Learners and Native Speakers

Katsunori Kotani
16-1 Nakamiyahigashino-cho, Hirakata,
Osaka, Japan 573-1001
kkotani@kansaigaidai.ac.jp

Takehiko Yoshimi
1-5 Yokotani, Seta, Otsu,
Shiga, Japan 520-7729
yoshimi@rins.ryukoku.ac.jp

Abstract

In order to develop effective computer-assisted language teaching systems for learners of English as a foreign language, it is first necessary to identify gaps between learners and native speakers in the four basic linguistic skills (reading, writing, pronunciation, and listening). To identify these gaps, the accuracy and fluency in language use between learners and native speakers should be compared using a learner corpus. However, previous corpora have not included all necessary types of linguistic data. Therefore, in this study, we aimed to design and build a new corpus comprising all types of linguistic data necessary for comparing accuracy and fluency in basic linguistic skills between learners and native speakers.

1 Introduction

Learners of English as a foreign language (EFL) frequently demonstrate a level of language ability that differs from that of native speakers (gap between learner and native speaker). Compared with native speakers, learners more frequently generate grammatically incorrect sentences and speak at a slower rate (Brand and Götz 2011, Chang 2012, Thewissen 2013). To develop tools and methods for effective learning of EFL, gaps in the four basic linguistic skills (reading, writing, pronunciation, and listening) need to be clearly identified and bridged.

A comparative learner corpus is a promising linguistic resource for identifying the gaps. To identify the gaps, a learner corpus should cover the basic linguistic skills (Treiman et al. 2003), because these skills are prerequisite for developing a level of ability adequate for effective communication with English speakers in a global society (Ono 2005).

A learner corpus should address gaps in both accuracy and fluency. Gaps in accuracy result from a lack of linguistic knowledge and manifest as misunderstandings when reading, grammatically incorrect usage when writing, mispronunciations when speaking, and misunderstandings when listening. Gaps in fluency result from a limited ability to perform cognitive-linguistic operations (Juffs and Rodríguez 2015), and manifest as slower rates of reading, writing, and pronunciation. In addition, fluency gaps also tend to result in a lack of confidence among learners.

Some learner corpora have been developed for the purpose of comparative analysis with native speakers (Sugiura 2007, Friginal et al. 2013, Barron and Black 2014); however, these corpora have only focused on writing and speaking, not reading or listening. A learner corpus compiled by Kotani et al. (2011) was composed of reading, writing, pronunciation, and listening data, but did not include data from native speakers.

In this study, we aimed to construct a comparative learner corpus to analyze gaps in the accuracy and fluency of the four basic linguistic skills. Specifically, this study collected corpus data from native speakers and merged these data with those from learners in the corpus compiled by Kotani et al. (2011). For this study, English speakers were categorized into four proficiency levels as follows: Learners in Kotani et al. (2011) were classified into three groups based on their level of proficiency, and native speakers were designated as the fourth and most advanced-level.

With the goal of supporting EFL teachers who use "authentic" materials such as web-pages that are used in English speakers' daily life, we also constructed a statistical model for calculating the

Short Paper Proceedings of the Eighth Workshop on Building and Using Comparable Corpora, pages 38–42,
Beijing, China, July 30, 2015. ©2015 Association for Computational Linguistics

difficulty of each sentence in authentic materials, which demonstrates the effectiveness of our corpus. Because the difficulty level of authentic materials is not always clear, teachers must personally inspect all such materials in order to verify that they are appropriate for the proficiency level of learners. Therefore, we developed a statistical model to automatically measure sentence difficulty and thereby reduce the effort required by teachers for this preparatory task.

2 Corpus between learners and native speakers

2.1 Corpus data

This study collected corpus data from native speakers following the method of Kotani et al. (2011). The corpus data of Kotani et al. (2011) consisted of data collected from learners for analyzing the accuracy and fluency of reading, writing, pronunciation, and listening, and the data are summarized in Table 1.

Language use	Perspective	
	Accuracy	Fluency
Reading	Comprehension rate	Silent-reading rate
		Difficulty judgment score
Writing	Written sentence (Correct rate)	Writing rate
		Difficulty judgment score
Pronunciation	Speech sound (Correct rate)	Reading-aloud rate
		Difficulty judgment score
Listening	Comprehension rate	Difficulty judgment score

Table 1: Summary of corpus data

The accuracy of reading (comprehension rate) was assessed by calculating the percentage of correct answers to comprehension questions based on written text. The accuracy of writing and pronunciation (the correct rate) was assessed by calculating the percentage of correctly written words or pronounced speech sounds from the total number of words in written sentences or spoken words, respectively. The accuracy of listening was assessed in terms of comprehension rate for spoken text, similarly to that of reading.

Fluency in terms of reading, writing, and pronunciation was assessed based on silent-reading, writing, and reading-aloud rates, respectively.

Fluency was also assessed based on a difficulty judgment score. Difficulty judgment scores for reading were assessed in terms of learners' judgment on the difficulty of reading comprehension, which they indicated on a five-point Likert scale (1: easy; 2: somewhat easy; 3: average; 4: somewhat difficult; or 5: difficult). Scores for writing were assessed in terms of learners' confidence in accuracy on a five-point Likert scale (1: confident; 2: somewhat confident; 3: average; 4: not very confident; or 5: not confident). Those for pronunciation and listening were assessed on the five-point Likert scale in terms of learners' judgment on the difficulty of pronunciation and listening comprehension, respectively.

2.2 Data collection method

Corpus data were collected through a series of reading, writing, pronunciation, and listening tasks. In the reading task, learners silently read 80 sentences in four news articles sentence-by-sentence, selected a difficulty score for each sentence, and answered five multiple-choice comprehension questions for each article. In the writing task, learners wrote sentences to describe four pictures and answered 20 questions about their background and computer skills, and then selected a difficulty score for each sentence. The pronunciation task proceeded similarly to the reading task: learners read aloud 80 sentences in four news articles, and selected a difficulty score for each sentence. Their voices were recorded in a sound-attenuated recording booth. In the listening task, similar to the reading task, learners listened to 80 sentences from four audio news clips sentence-by-sentence, and then selected a difficulty score for each sentence. After a clip was finished, the learner answered five multiple-choice comprehension questions for each clip.

The learner corpus of Kotani et al. (2011) compiled corpus data from three different proficiency groups of learners (beginner-level, intermediate-level, and advanced-level) based on TOEIC (Test of English for International Communication) scores; each group comprised 30 learners. Hence, for this study, we chose to collect corpus data from 30 native speakers (16 male, 14 female; mean age ± standard deviation [SD], 22.5 ± 2.0 years; age range, 20–27 years) to represent a level higher than that of advanced-level learners. The native speakers were recruited from among university students living in areas in and around Tokyo. All native speakers were compensated for their participation.

2.3 Descriptive statistics

All distributions shown in Tables 2, 3, and 4 followed our expectation that the difficulty of a task would decrease from the beginner to the native speaker level. This outcome suggests the validity of our corpus data.

Mean comprehension rates (± SD) of 120 instances collected from each group (n = 30) of learners and native speakers in four articles and clips involving the reading and listening tasks, are summarized in Table 2.

Group	Task	
	Reading	Listening
Beginner	47.3(23.6)	43.3(22.2)
Intermediate	52.0(22.7)	49.8(20.9)
Advanced	65.8(24.0)	67.0(20.0)
Native-speaker	76.5(21.8)	75.7(17.4)

Table 2: Comprehension rates of the four groups (%); mean (SD)

Group	Task			
	Reading	Writing	Pronunciation	Listening
Beginner	3.26 (0.84)	3.07 (0.94)	3.61 (0.89)	3.63 (0.76)
Intermediate	2.72 (0.81)	3.02 (0.60)	3.29 (0.80)	3.18 (0.72)
Advanced	2.18 (0.92)	2.36 (1.00)	2.73 (1.05)	2.28 (0.96)
Native-speaker	1.92 (0.84)	1.56 (0.73)	2.15 (0.88)	1.87 (0.82)

Table 3: Difficulty judgment scores of the four groups; mean (SD)

Mean difficulty judgment scores (± SD) of 2400 instances collected from each group (n = 30) in 80 sentences involving reading task, are summarized in Table 3. Mean difficulty judgment scores (± SD) of 30*m instances collected from each group (n = 30) in m sentences involving the writing task, in which the number of written sentences (m) differed for each individual, are also summarized in Table 3. Mean difficulty judgment scores (± SD) of 2400 instances collected from each group (n = 30) in 80 sentences involving pronunciation and listening tasks, are also shown.

Mean processing rates (± SD) of 2400 instances collected from each group in 80 sentences involving reading task, are summarized in Table 4. Mean writing rates (± SD) of 30*l instances collected from each group (n = 30) in l sentences involving the writing task, in which the number of written sentences (l) differed for each individual, are also summarized in Table 4. Mean processing rates (± SD) of 2400 instances collected from each group in 80 sentences involving pronunciation task, are also shown. Processing rates were calculated as the number of words read/written/pronounced in one minute (WPM: words per minute).

Group	Task		
	Reading	Writing	Pronunciation
Beginner	86.91 (42.19)	9.21 (3.50)	66.28 (13.10)
Intermediate	97.17 (32.11)	10.21 (3.96)	76.97 (15.27)
Advanced	128.32 (44.99)	13.35 (5.42)	91.68 (12.87)
Native-speaker	206.21 (61.15)	17.34 (5.78)	119.91 (14.73)

Table 4: Processing rates of the four groups (WPM); mean (SD)

3 Measurement of sentence difficulty

3.1 Goal

In order to select online materials that are appropriate for the proficiency level of learners, a teacher must personally assess the difficulty of the materials, which is often unclear. A method that would enable the automatic measuring of sentence difficulty of online materials would thereby be expected to reduce the burden of this preparatory task.

To achieve this, we constructed a statistical model based on our corpus data. Our statistical model calculates sentence difficulty in terms of gaps in language use between learners and native speakers on the basis of linguistic features of sentences.

3.2 Methods

We carried out a multiple regression analysis of our corpus data using sentence length (number of words), and mean length of words in a sentence (mean number of syllables), as independent variables.

For the dependent variable, we used the gaps in the silent-reading rate, which were derived for each sentence (n = 80) by subtracting the mean silent-reading rate of advanced-level learners (n = 30) from that of native speakers (n = 30). The distribution of these gaps is summarized in Figure 1. The gaps ranged from < 25 to > 125 WPM, and the distribution of silent-reading rates followed a normal distribution according to the Kolmogorov-Smirnov test (K = 0.49, $p < 0.01$).

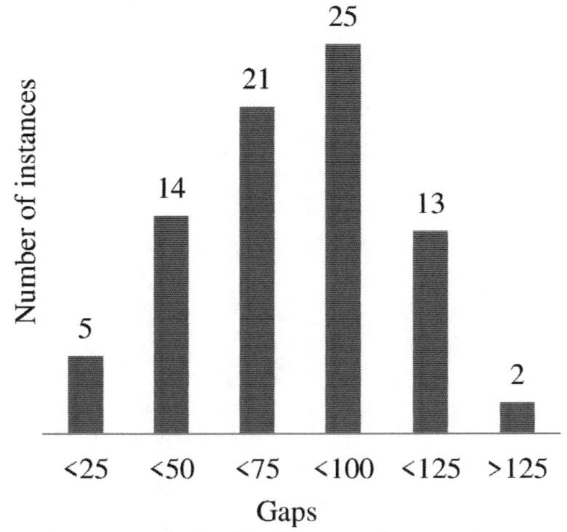

Figure 1: Gaps in the silent-reading rate between learners and native speakers (WPM)

3.3 Results

A significant relationship was observed between the linear combination of linguistic features and gaps in the silent-reading rate ($F(2, 77) = 17.42$, $p < 0.01$). The sample multiple correlation coefficient adjusted for degrees of freedom was 0.54, indicating that approximately 31.1% of the variance in the gaps in the sample could be accounted for by the linear combination of linguistic features.

We then assessed our method using a leave-one-out cross-validation test. In this test, our method was examined n times (n = 80) by using one instance as test data and $n-1$ instances as training data. Spearman's correlation coefficient was used to compare the gaps predicted using our method with those that were actually measured. The correlation coefficient ($r = 0.48$) was statistically significantly different from zero ($p <$ 0.01).

Errors in the cross-validation test results are summarized in Figure 2. Errors were calculated as absolute values of the differences between gaps predicted using our method and the actual gaps. Our method was associated with a lower error rate (0 to 25 WPM).

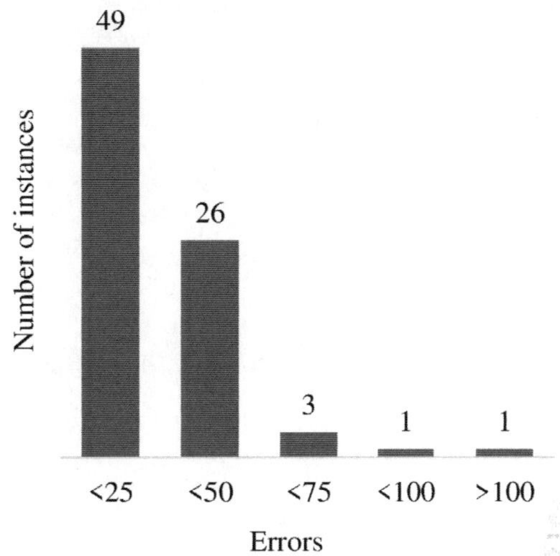

Figure 2: Errors in the cross-validation test results (WPM)

4 Conclusion

This paper described the construction of a corpus comprising all types of linguistic data necessary for comparing accuracy and fluency in basic linguistic skills between learners and native speakers. We expect that this corpus will enable teachers to more accurately assess the performance of learners in greater detail through a comparison with native speakers. We also expect our statistical model to serve as an effective method for measuring the difficulty of online materials, thereby reducing the burden of this preparatory task and allowing teachers to more easily select online materials that are appropriate for the proficiency level of learners.

Acknowledgments

This work was supported in part by Grant-in-Aid for Scientific Research (B) (22300299) and (15H02940).

Reference

Christiane Brand and Sandra Götz. 2011. Fluency versus accuracy in advanced spoken learner language. *Errors and Disfluencies in Spoken Corpora. Special Issue of International Journal of Corpus Linguistics*, 16(2): 255–275.

Anne Barron and Emily Black. 2014. Constructing small talk in learner-native speaker voice-based telecollaboration: A focus on topic management and backchanneling. *System*, 48: 112-128.

Anna C.-S. Chang. 2012. Improving reading rate activities for EFL students: Timed reading and repeated oral reading. *Reading in a Foreign Language*, 24(1): 56-83.

Eric Friginal, Man Li, and Sara C. Weigle. 2013. Revisiting multiple profiles of learner compositions: A comparison of highly rated NS and NNS essays. *Journal of Second Language Writing*, .23: 1-16.

Alan Juffs and Guillermo A. Rodríguez. 2015. *Second Language Sentence Processing*. New York: Routledge.

Katsunori Kotani, Takehiko Yoshimi, Hiroaki Nanjo, and Hitoshi Isahara. 2011. Compiling learner corpus data of linguistic output and language processing in speaking, listening, writing, and reading. *Proceedings of the 5th International Joint Conference on Natural Language Processing (IJCNLP 2011):* 1418-1422.

Hiroshi Ono. 2005. A development of placement test and e-learning system for Japanese university students: Research on support improving academic ability based on IT. *Research Report, National Institute of Multimedia Education 2005-6*.

Jennifer Thewissen. 2013. Capturing L2 accuracy developmental patterns: Insights from an error-tagged EFL learner corpus. *The Modern Language Journal*, 97(1): 77–101.

Rebecca Treiman, Charles Clifton Jr., Antje S. Meyer, and Lee H. Wurm. 2003. Language comprehension and production. *Comprehensive Handbook of Psychology 4: Experimental Psychology*. New York: John Wiley & Sons, Inc.: 527-548.

Masatoshi Sugiura, Masumi Narita, Tomomi Ishida, Tatsuya Sakaue, Remi Murao, and Kyoko Muraki. 2007. A discriminant analysis of non-native speakers and native speakers of English. *Proceedings of the 2007 Corpus Linguistics Conference*.

A Generative Model for Extracting Parallel Fragments from Comparable Documents

Somayeh Bakhshaei[1], Shahram Khadivi[2*] and Reza Safabakhsh[1]
[1]Computer Engineering Department, Amirkabir University of Technology, Tehran, Iran
[2]eBay Inc., Aachen, Germany
bakhshaei@aut.ac.ir, skhadivi@ebay.com, safa@aut.ac.ir

Abstract

Although parallel corpora are essential language resources for many NLP tasks, they are rare or even not available for many language pairs. Instead, comparable corpora are widely available and contain parallel fragments of information that can be used applications like statistical machine translations. In this research, we propose a generative LDA based model for extracting parallel fragments from comparable documents without using any initial parallel data or bilingual lexicon. The experimental results show significant improvement if the extracted sentence fragments generated by the proposed method are used in addition to an existing parallel corpus in an SMT task. According to human judgment, the accuracy of the proposed method for an English-Persian task is about 66%. Also, the OOV rate for the same task is reduced by 28%.

1 Introduction

Parallel corpora are essential for many applications like statistical machine translation (SMT). Even resource rich language pairs in terms of parallel corpora always need more data, since languages evolve and diversify over time. Comparable corpora are considered as a widely available language resource that contains notably large amount of parallel sentence fragments. However, mining these fragments is a challenging task, and therefore many different approaches were proposed to extract parallel sentences, parallel fragments, or parallel lexicon. It has been shown in the previous works that extracting parallel sentences from comparable corpora usually results in a noisy parallel corpus (Munteanu & Marcu, 2006). Since comparable documents rarely contain exact parallel sentences, instead they contain a good amount of parallel sub-sentences or fragments. Thus, it is better to search for parallel fragments instead of parallel sentences.

Recent research works in fragment extraction have shown significant improvements in SMT quality, if parallel fragments are also used in the training phase (Chiao & Zweigenbaum, 2002; Déjean, et al., 2002; Fung & McKeown, 1997; Fung & Yee, 1998; Gupta, et al., 2013; Otero, P. G, 2007; Rapp, R., 1999; Saralegui, et al. 2008). In this work, we also focus on extracting parallel fragments from comparable corpora. Our proposed approach is a generative model based on latent Dirichlet allocation (LDA) principles (Blei & Jordan, 2003).

In our proposed generative model, we assume there are parallel topics as hidden variables that model the parallel fragments in a comparable document corpus. We define parallel fragments as a sequence of occurrence of one of these parallel topics. This sequence occurs densely on a pair of comparable documents. It is possible to consider more than one topic in the structure of topic sequence but in this work we have limited it to one for simplicity and lower computational complexities. Considering more topics in the structure of a sequence that produces parallel fragments is suggested as our future work.

The rest of the paper is organized as follows. Section 2 describes the related works. Section 3 describes the generative process for producing comparable documents. The model architecture is described in section 4 with a graphical model. Section 5 describes the data, tools and resources

* This work has been done when Shahram Khadivi was with Amirkabir University of Technology.

Long Paper Proceedings of the Eighth Workshop on Building and Using Comparable Corpora, pages 43–51,
Beijing, China, July 30, 2015. ©2015 Association for Computational Linguistics

used for this work and then the experiments and evaluation results are presented. Section 6 concludes and presents avenues for future works.

2 Related works

Comparable corpora are useful resources for many research fields of NLP. Also, SMT as one of the major problems of the NLP field can benefit from comparable corpora. Previous researches have suggested different approaches for extracting parallel information from comparable corpora. The main approaches are categorized as: **Lexicon Induction, Wikipedia based, Bridge Language, Graph based, Bootstrapping** and **EM**.

Works that are reported for **Lexicon Induction** are almost focused on extracting words from comparable corpora. These works use different methods that we categorize as: Seed based, model based and graph based methods.

The aim of the **Seed based Lexicon Induction** approach is expanding an initial parallel seed. Most of these researches use the context vector idea (Fung & Yee, 1998; Irvine & Callison-Burch, 2013; Rapp, 1995; Rapp, R., 1999). Gaussier, et al. (2004) proposes a geometric model for finding the synonym words in the space of the context vectors. Garera, et al. (2009) defines context vectors on the dependency tree rather than using adjacency. Some works use specific features for describing words like temporal co-occurrences (Schafer & Yarowsky, 2002), linguistic features (Kholy, et al., 2013; Koehn & Knight, 2002), and web based visual similarity features (Bergsma & Van Durme, 2011; Fiser & Ljubesic, 2011). The suggested features are almost efficient for similar or closely related languages but not all of the language pairs.

The **Model based Lexicon Induction** approach contains works that suggest a model for extracting parallel words. (Daumé III & Jagarlamudi, 2011; Haghighi, et al., 2008) use a generative model based on Canonical Correlation Analysis (CCA) (Hardoon, et al., 2004). They assume that by mapping words to a feature space, similar words are located in a subspace which is called the latent space of common concepts. Although their model is strong, they have defined it based on orthographical features (in addition to context vectors) that reduce the efficiency of the model for nonrelated languages. Diab & Finch (2000) also defines a matching function on similar words of languages. They assume that for two synonyms with close distributional profiles, the distributional profile of their corresponding translation should also be correlated in a comparable corpus. The optimization phase of the model that is based on gradient descent is very complex and time complexity is the biggest challenge of this model facing big data. The experiment is restricted to highly frequent words. Quirk, et al. (2007) also proposes a generative model. Their model is a developed version of IBM 1, 2 models. Although these are generative models for extracting parallel fragments, they completely differ from our model. Our model is based on the LDA model and we define a simpler but more efficient model with an accurate probabilistic distribution for parallel fragments in comparable corpora.

Wikipedia as a multilingual encyclopedia is a rich source of multilingual comparable corpora. There are lots of works reported in the **Wikipedia based** researches (Otero & López, 2010). Otero & López (2010) download the entire Wikipedia for any two languages, makes the "CorpusPedia", and then extracts information from this corpus. However, in recent works it is shown that only a small ad-hoc corpus containing Wikipedia articles can be beneficial for an existing MT system (Pal, et al., 2014). Although the Wikipedia based approach is a successful method for producing parallel information, the limitation of Wikipedia articles for most of the language pairs is a big problem.

The methods of Cross-lingual Information Retrieval are widely used for mining comparable corpora. The **Bridge language** idea is specially used for extracting parallel information between languages (Gispert & Mario, 2006; Kumar, et al., 2007; Mann & Yarowsky, 2001; Wu & Wang, 2007). Some papers use multiple languages for pivoting (Soderland, et al., 2009). The big problem of this approach is its unavoidable noisy output. Thus some other papers use a two-step version of this model for solving the problem. They first produce output and then refine it by removing its noise (Shezaf & Rappoport, 2010; Kaji, et al., 2008).

A wide range of researches are using a **Graph** for extracting parallel information from comparable corpora. Laws, et al., (2010) make a graph on the source (src) and target (trg) words (nodes are considered as src/trg words) and finds the similar nodes using the SimRank idea (Jeh & Widom, 2002). Some works define an optimization problem for finding the similarity on the edges of the graph of src and trg words (Muthukrishnan, et al., 2011). Razmara, et al.,

(2013) and Saluja & Navrátil, (2013) use graphs for solving the out-of-vocabulary (OOV) error in MT. Razmara, et al. (2013) make the nodes of the graph on phrases in addition to words. Minkov & Cohen (2012) use words and their stems for his graph nodes, and also the dependency tree for preserving the structure of words in source and target sentences. Some other works use the simple but efficient **EM** algorithm for producing a bilingual lexicon (Koehn & Knight, 2000).

A wide range of bootstraps are applied for extracting bilingual information from comparable corpora. Two-level approaches starts with (Munteanu & Marcu, 2006) that changes a sentence to a signal, based on LLR score and then uses a filter for extracting parallel fragments. This approach is continued in the latter works (Xiang, et al., 2013). Chu, et al. (2013) use the similar idea on quasi–comparable corpora. Klementiev, et al. (2012) use a heuristic approach for making context vectors directly on parallel phrases instead of parallel words. (Aker & Gaizauskas, 2012; Hewavitharana & Vogel, 2013) define a classifier for extracting parallel fragments.

3 LDA Based Generative Model

For extracting parallel fragments we use the LDA concept (Blei & Jordan, 2003). The base of our model is a bilingual topic model. Bilingual topic models were studied in previous works. Multilingual topic models similar to this work were presented in (Ni, et al., 2009) and (Mimno, et al., 2009). However, their models are polylingual topic models that are trained on words and our model is the extended version of this type of models but with additional capability of producing parallel fragments. In (Boyd-Graber J. a., 2009) a bilingual topic model is presented. The model is trained on a pair of src and trg words which are prepared by a matching function while training topic models. Another proposed model is (Boyd-Graber & P. Resnik, 2010) that is a customized version of LDA for sentimental analysis.

We infer topics as distributions over words as usual in topic model but the model is biased to a specific distribution of topics over words of documents. We assume that a pair of comparable documents is made of a topic distribution. We define topics over words but only the topics that are proper for producing parallel fragments are chosen. Therefore we limit them to ones that produce a dense bilingual sequence of source and target words in a comparable document pair. We use a definite function for controlling the topics and producing parallel fragments; this function is called $m()$. Function m accepts pairs of fragments, $\langle f^s, f^t \rangle$, if Conditions (1) satisfies and rejects them otherwise. The graphical presentation of proposed model is depicted in Figure 1. Model variables and relations are also shown in the figure. Here, we have used a known variable m.

Each pair of comparable documents will be generated with the generative process of Table 1. In this process β^s, β^t and α are hyper-parameters of the Dirichlet distributions. Topic distribution ϕ^t and ϕ^s is drawn from $Dir(\beta^t)$ & $Dir(\beta^s)$ respectively. First a sample distribution $\theta \sim Dir(\alpha)$ is drawn for both source and target document. Then each word of the comparable document pair is drawn from a multinomial distribution parameterized with θ, $z \sim Mult(\theta)$. Source and target words are generated from the respective topic distribution: $w^* \sim \phi^*_{w^*|z}$.

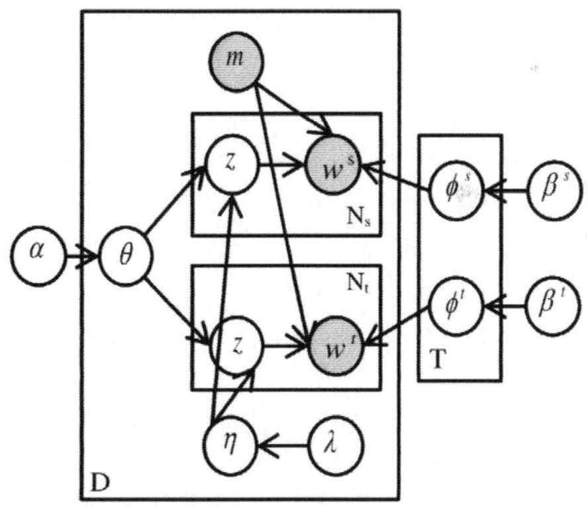

Figure 1: Graphical model for extracting parallel fragments. Function m determines if the assigned sequence of topics to the observed fragments satisfies Conditions (1). If so, the parallel pair of source and target fragments will be produced.

According to the given definition for parallel fragments in section 1, we produce a dense sequence of topics. In fact, by a dense sequence of a topic we mean a sub sentence of source and target document with limited length in which most of its words come from one topic distribution. For controlling these sub-sentences, we define the following conditions:

1. Length of the fragments is limited,
2. At least 50% of the words of a valid fragment come from one specific topic.

We refer to these conditions as Conditions (1) in the rest of the paper.

1. *Sample source & target topic distributions:*
$\phi^s \sim Dir(\beta^s)$, $\phi^t \sim Dir(\beta^t)$,
2. *For each document pair* $D = < S, T >$,
a) *Sample a topic distribution:* $\theta \sim Dir(\alpha)$,
b) *Sample the length of parallel fragments:*
$\eta \sim Poisson(\lambda)$,
c) *Produce* η *random indexes from* S & T,
d) *Sample a topic* $z' \sim Mult(\theta)$,
e) *Sample each of the chosen indexes:*
$w^* \sim \phi_{w^*|z'}$,
f) *Sample the rest of indexes:*
$z \sim Mult(\theta), w^* \sim \phi_{w^*|z}$,
g) *If sequence of chosen topics satisfies conditions(1):*
produce parallel fragments.

Table 1: Generative model for producing comparable document corpus.

4 Inference

Given a corpus of comparable documents our goal is to infer the unknown parameters of the model. According to Figure 2 we infer topics ϕ^t and ϕ^s, distribution of parallel topics on the source and target documents, θ and topic assignment z.

We use a collapsed Gibbs sampler (Neal, 2000) for sampling the latent variable of topic assignment z. We use two sets *I* and *J*. These two sets are random indexes chosen from source and target word indexes of the source and target documents, respectively:

$$\{I\}_1^\eta = Rand(N_{d,s})$$

$$\{J\}_1^\eta = Rand(N_{d,t})$$

The size of these two sets is defined based on the maximum length of parallel fragments in each document pair. The maximum length of parallel fragments, η, is randomly sampled from a Poisson distribution, $Poisson(\lambda)$:

$$\eta \sim Poisson(\lambda)$$

The words that appear in the indexes of sets I and J are respectively shown as *w(I)* and *w(J)*. Words of these two sets are made from one topic and build the dense sequence of words. We set $N_k^{w(I)}$ *and* $N_k^{w(J)}$ as the number of assignment of topic k to the source and target words, $w(I)$ *and* $w(J)$, occurring in the words indexes of the sets *I* and *J*. Also $N_{I,-i}^k$ *and* $N_{J,-i}^k$ are the number of times topic *k* occurs in the indexes defined in *I* and *J* sets in the source and target documents.

$$p(z_i = k \mid z_{-i}, I, J, \phi^s, \phi^t) = p(I \mid z_i = k, \phi^s, z_{-i}) p(\phi^s)$$
$$p(J \mid z_i = k, \phi^t, z_{-i}) p(\phi^t)$$
$$\approx \frac{N_{k,-i}^{w(I)} + \beta^s}{\sum_n N_{k,-i}^n + \beta^s} \frac{N_{I,-i}^k + \beta^s}{\sum_n N_{I,-i}^n + \beta^s} \times$$
$$\frac{N_{k,-i}^{w(J)} + \beta^t}{\sum_n N_{k,-i}^n + \beta^t} \frac{N_{J,-i}^k + \beta^t}{\sum_n N_{J,-i}^n + \beta^t}$$

We assume source and target words that are located in the current index i, w_i^s *and* w_i^t, are a member of $w(I)$ *and* $w(J)$ respectively, but while we are generating a word index outside *I* and *J*, then $N_k^{w(I)}$ *and* $N_k^{w(J)}$ changes to $N_k^{w_i}$ *and* $N_k^{w_j}$.

Finally function $m()$ produces parallel fragments $< f^s, f^t >$ only if they are consistent with Conditions (1) defined in Section 3.

Corpus		#Documents	#Words
Raw_ccNews	en	194K	47M
	fa	194K	42M
Refined_ccNews	en	97K	29M
	fa	97K	23M

Table 2: Statistics of used comparable corpora. The number of documents and running words is reported for each side of the corpus.

	Side	#Fragments	#Words
Extracted parallel fragments	en	75K	416K
	fa	75K	448K

Table 3: Statistic of extracted parallel fragments.

5 Experimental Setup

We have two strategies for evaluating our model. In the first step we try to measure the quality of extracted fragments from comparable documents. In the other scenario we evaluate the quality of the extracted parallel fragment by evaluating the quality of the SMT system equipped with this extra information.

5.1 Data

The data we use is a corpus of comparable documents, ccNews. The languages of these data are Farsi (fa) and English (en). The domain of these documents is News gathered between years 2007

#	src/trg	Worse parallel fragment samples	Error type
1	En	permanent security council members	Type 1.1 in target fragment.
	Fa	شورای دایم سازمان امنیت	
	En CT	permanent security council	
2	En	nobel peace prize winner	Type 1.2 in target fragment.
	Fa	برنده هندی جایزه صلح نوبل	
	En CT	indian nobel peace prize winner	
3	En	official irna news agency	Type 2.
	Fa	خبرگزاری نیمه رسمی فارس	
	En CT	official fars news agency	
4	En	eu foreign	Type 1.1 in source fragment.
	Fa	مسئول سیاست خارجی اتحادیه اروپا	
	En CT	eu foreign policy chief	
5	En	unanimously adopted the resolution imposing sanctions	Type 3.
	Fa	شورای امنیت سازمان ملل روز شنبه به اتفاق آرا	
	En CT	the un security council on saturday unanimously	

Table 4: Some worse parallel fragments produced by our model are recognized by manually checking the model output. The errors are highlighted and the correct translation of English part for the extracted Farsi fragment is written in EnCT row.

to 2010. The raw version of this corpus (Raw_ccNews) has about 193K documents and about 47M and 42M words, respectively in en and fa sides. We did some refinement on the corpus and the result is named Refined_ccNews corpus, as seen in Table 2. We removed repeated documents and also pairs of documents with incompatible ratio of words are removed.

The incompatibility of words ratio is defined as the proportion of words of one side to the other side. This ratio is set to be in the interval [0.5, 2]. That is:

$$0.5 \leq \frac{\#words\ of\ source\ side\ document}{\#words\ of\ target\ side\ document} \leq 2$$

The full information of the corpus is reported in Table 2.

5.2 Topic Model Parameters

In the experiments the hyper-parameter of the model are manually set to β^s, β^t=0.8 and $\alpha = 1$. And the number of topics in the models is set to T=800. The side effect of the training model is a parallel topic model. These topics are those that have common words with the source and target side of at least one comparable document pair. The iteration of Gibbs sampling is set to 1000.

The parallel fragments of the last iteration produced by $m()$ function are reported as the final result.

5.3 Results Analysis

The statistic of extracted parallel fragments is reported in Table 3. On average, 75K parallel fragments are extracted from 97K comparable documents. These numbers show that the model just produces high confidence samples and ignores most of them.

Evaluation Strategy 1 - According to our knowledge there is no criterion to automatically evaluate the quality of extracted data. Thus for evaluating the quality of the results we use human judgment. We asked a human translator familiar with both Farsi and English languages to check the quality of the parallelized fragments and mark the pairs that are wrongly parallelized and to write down a definition of the occurred error.

The results of manually checking the extracted fragments are shown in Table 4. In this table we have reported some of the worst errors of the model.

According to human judge, we recognized some specific types of error in the model output. These errors are categorized into three types:

1. Wrong boundaries for parallel fragments,
    1.1. Tighter boundaries that lead to incomplete phrases,
    1.2. Wider boundaries that lead to additional wrong tokens in the start/end of parallel fragments.
2. Same class words that are not the exact translation of each other.

3. Completely wrong samples,

Type 1 error is related to the samples in which boundaries are not correctly chosen by the model. This type is separated into two sub parts for tighter or wider boundaries which respectively ignores or adds some key tokens to the parallel fragments which leads to error.

Type 2 errors are produced because of using co-class words instead of synonyms. This is because the model intentionally groups words based on co-occurrence instead of considering meaning which it has inherited from the LDA base of the model (the model is actually a topic model and this is a usual behavior of topic models). This bug of the model can be considered as future works for improving the model accuracy.

At the end, the reason for Type 3 errors is not obviously known. These samples are produced because of the inner noises of the model. We guess these are the unavoidable noises of comparable documents that are extended to the model output.

According to this classification of errors, the proportion of each error type is computed. The results are reported in Table 5. These are the proportion of each type observed in a set of 400 random fragments which is evaluated by human translator. The most observed error is related to type 1. Thus the human evaluation suggests 66% accuracy for the model output.

Evaluation Strategy 2 – In the second step, for evaluating the model output, we consider the effect of these extracted data in the quality of an existing SMT system. For this aim, at first we train a base line system on a parallel corpus. Our corpus is the Mizan parallel corpus[2]. The domain of this corpus is literature. For challenging the translation system, we used an out-of-domain test. Our test is selected from the news domain.

The standard phrase-based decoder that we use for training models is the Moses system (Koehn, et al., 2007) in which we use default values for all of the decoder parameters. We also use a 4-gram language model trained using SRILM (Stolcke, 2002) with Kneser-Ney smoothing (Kneser & Ney, 1995). To tune the decoder's feature weights with minimum error rate (Och, 2003), we use a development (dev) set of 1000 single-reference sentences, and we evaluate the models performance on a test set of 1032 multiple-references sentences. For more information on the data see Table 6. Domain of the dev set and training corpus is literature while the test set domain is news.

As it is seen in Table 7, different approaches are proposed for how to use parallel fragments for improving the baseline system. Description of the models is explained in the follow.

Baseline - This is an SMT system that is trained on main corpus (Mizan). The BLEU score of the baseline system is 10.41% on dev and 8.01% on test set. The OOV error in this system is 3509 and 768 on test and dev sets respectively.

Baseline+ParallelFragments - In this system we directly add the parallel fragments to our main corpus and train a new system. The BLEU score improvement is about 0.27% and 0.22% respectively on test and dev sets. OOV error reduces too.

Baseline+ParallelFragments (Giza weightes) - This approach is the same as **Baseline+ParallelFragments** but we use the weighted corpus for Giza alignment. The weight of main corpus and parallel fragments is set to 10 and 1 respectively.

BaseLine+PT_ParallelFragments - In this approach we combine the phrase tables of baseline and the system trained on parallel fragments. Actually because of the difference domain of main corpus and parallel fragments, it is expected that combining these two resources harm the quality of the baseline system. So, we use the phrase table which is trained on parallel fragments as the back off for the phrase table of the baseline system. The results show significant improvement in this case. The BLEU score improves by about 1% on test set and OOV error is decreased by 28%.

Thus, the results shown in Table 7 reveals that the extracted parallel fragments can improve the quality of the translation output.

Error Type	P
Type 1	33%
Type 2	0.04%
Type 3	0.02%

Table 5: Analysis of model output base of error types recognized by human translator judgment.

[2] Supreme Council of Information and Communication Technology. (2013). Mizan English-Persian Parallel Corpus. Tehran, I.R. Iran. Retrieved from http://dadegan.ir/catalog/mizan.

6 Conclusion

In this paper we have proposed a generative LDA based model for extracting parallel fragments from comparable corpora. The main contribution of the proposed model is that it is developed for extracting parallel fragments from comparable documents corpus without the need to any parallel data such as initial seed or dictionary.

We have evaluated the output of the model by using a human translator judgment and also by using the extracted data for expanding the training data set of a SMT system. Results of the augmented system show improvement of the output quality.

The result of human judgment categorizes the dominant errors of the model to three types. Most errors are related to the wrong recognized boundaries by the model. We have considered the refinement of these kinds of errors as our future works. We have also shown that the model is able to reduce the OOV error.

			#Line	#Words	Domain
Train	en		1021323	13636292	Literature
	fa		1021323	13686642	
Test	en		1032	28112	News
	fa	1	1032	30451	
		2	1032	33725	
		3	1032	33128	
		4	1032	32417	
Dev	en		1000	23055	Literature
	fa		1000	26351	

Table 6: Statistic of Train, Test and Dev set for making the SMT system.

SMT system	Test		Dev	
	BLEU (%)	OOV	BLEU (%)	OOV
Baseline	10.41	3509	8.01	768
+ParallelFragments	10.68	2459	8.22	737
+ ParallelFragments (Giza weighted)	10.53	2460	8.23	737
+PT_ParallelFragm ents	**11.46**	2530	8.14	734

Table 7: Results of trained SMT systems.

References

Aker, A., & Gaizauskas, Y. F. (2012). Automatic bilingual phrase extraction from comparable corpora. *Proceedings of COLING 2012: Posters* (pp. 23–32). COLING 2012, Mumbai.

Bergsma, S., & Van Durme, B. (2011). Learning bilingual lexicons using the visual similarity of labeled web images. *In IJCAI Proceedings-International Joint Conference on Artificial Intelligence*, (pp. Vol. 22, No. 3, p. 1764).

Blei, D. M., & Jordan, M. I. (2003). Latent dirichlet allocation. *the Journal of machine Learning research*, 3, 993-1022.

Boyd-Graber, J. a. (2009). Multilingual topic models for unaligned text. *In Proceedings of the Twenty-Fifth Conference on Uncertainty in Artificial Intelligence* (pp. 75-82). AUAI Press.

Boyd-Graber, J., & P. Resnik. (2010). Holistic sentiment analysis across languages: Multilingual supervised latent Dirichlet allocation. *In Proceedings of the 2010 Conference on EMNLP*, (pp. 45-55).

Chiao, Y. C., & Zweigenbaum, P. (2002). Looking for candidate translational equivalents in specialized, comparable corpora. *In Proceedings of the 19th international conference on Computational linguistics-Volume 2*, (pp. 1-5).

Chu, C., Nakazawa, T., & Kurohashi, S. (2013). Accurate Parallel Fragment Extraction from Quasi–Comparable Corpora using Alignment Model and Translation Lexicon. *Proceedings of the Sixth International Joint Conference on Natural Language Processing*, (pp. 1144--1150).

Daumé III, H., & Jagarlamudi, J. (2011). Domain adaptation for machine translation by mining unseen words. *Proceedings of the 49th Annual Meeting of the Association for Computational Linguistics: Human Language Technologies: short papers-Volume 2*. Association for Computational Linguistics.

Déjean, H., Gaussier, É., & Sadat, F. (2002). Bilingual terminology extraction: an approach based on a multilingual thesaurus applicable to comparable corpora. *In Proceedings of the 19th International Conference on Computational Linguistics COLING.*

Diab, M., & Finch, S. (2000). *A statistical word-level translation model for comparable corpora.* IN PROCEEDINGS OF THE CONFERENCE ON CONTENT-BASED MULTIMEDIA INFORMATION ACCESS (RIAO).

Fiser, D., & Ljubesic, N. (2011). Bilingual lexicon extraction from comparable corpora for closely related languages. *In RANLP*, 125-131.

Fung, P., & McKeown, K. (1997). Finding terminology translations from non-parallel corpora. *In Proceedings of the 5th Annual Workshop on Very Large Corpora*, (pp. 192-202).

Fung, P., & Yee, L. Y. (1998). An ir approach for translating new words from nonparallel, comparable texts. *In Proceedings of the 36th Annual Meeting of the Association and 17th International Conference on Computational Linguistics - Volume 1, ACL '98* (pp. 414-420). Association for Computational Linguistics.

Garera, N., Callison-Burch, C., & Yarowsky, D. (2009). Improving translation lexicon induction from monolingual corpora via dependency contexts and part-of-speech equivalences. *Proceedings of the Thirteenth Conference on Computational Natural Languag Learning.* Association for Computational Linguistic.

Gaussier, E., Renders, J. M., Matveeva, I., Goutte, C., & Déjean, H. (2004). A geometric view on bilingual lexicon extraction from comparable corpora. *In Proceedings of the 42nd Annual Meeting on ACL*, (p. 526).

Gispert, A. d., & Mario, B. (2006). Catalan-english statistical machine translation without parallel corpus: bridging through spanish. *in Proc. of 5th International Conference on Language Resources and Evaluation (LREC).* Genoa, Italy.

Gupta, R., Pal, S., & Bandyopadhyay, S. (2013). Improving mt system using extracted parallel fragments of text from comparable corpora. *In proceedings of 6th workshop of BUCC, ACL, Sofia, Bulgaria*, (pp. 69-76).

Haghighi, A., Liang, P., Berg-Kirkpatrick, T., & Klein, D. (2008). Learning Bilingual Lexicons from Monolingual Corpora. *In ACL, Vol. 2008*, (pp. 771-779).

Hardoon, D. R., Szedmak, S., & Shawe-Taylor, J. (2004). Canonical correlation analysis: An overview with application to learning methods. *Neural Computation 16.12*, 2639-2664.

Hewavitharana, S., & Vogel, S. (2013). Extracting parallel phrases from comparable data. *Building and Using Comparable Corpora. Springer Berlin Heidelberg*, 191-204.

Irvine, A., & Callison-Burch, C. (2013). Supervised bilingual lexicon induction with multiple monolingual signals. *Proceedings of NAACL-HLT.*

Jeh, G., & Widom, J. (2002). Simrank: A measure of structural-context similarity. *In KDD '02*, pages 538–543.

Kaji, H., Tamamura, S., & Erdenebat, D. (2008). Automatic construction of a japanese-chinese dictionary via english. *In LREC.*

Kholy, E., Nizar Habash, A., Leusch, G., Matusov, E., & Sawaf, H. (2013). Language independent connectivity strength features for phrase pivot statistical machine translation. In Proc. of ACL, vol. 13.

Klementiev, A., Irvine, A., Callison-Burch, C., & Yarowsky, D. (2012). Toward statistical machine translation without parallel corpora. *In Proceedings of the 13th Conference of the European Chapter of the ACL*, (pp. 130-140).

Kneser, R., & Ney, H. (1995). Improved backing-off for m-gram language modeling. *In Acoustics, Speech, and Signal Processing, 1995. ICASSP-95., 1995 International Conference on Vol. 1*, (pp. 181-184). IEEE.

Koehn, P., & Knight, K. (2000). Estimating word translation probabilities from unrelated monolingual corpora using the EM algorithm. *AAAI/IAAI.*

Koehn, P., & Knight, K. (2002). Learning a translation lexicon from monolingual corpora. *Proceedings of the ACL-02 workshop on Unsupervised lexical acquisition-Volume 9.* Association for Computational Linguistics.

Koehn, P., Hoang, H., Birch, A., Callison-Burch, C., Federico, M., Bertoldi, N., et al. (2007). Moses: Open source toolkit for statistical machine translation. *In Proceedings of the 45th annual meeting of the ACL on interactive poster and demonstration sessions*, (pp. 177-180).

Kumar, S., Och, F. J., & Macherey, W. (2007). Improving Word Alignment with Bridge Languages. *EMNLP-CoNLL.*

Laws, F., Michelbacher, L., Dorow, B., Scheible, C., Heid, U., & Schütze, H. (2010). A linguistically grounded graph model for bilingual lexicon extraction. *In Proceedings of the 23rd International Conference on Computational Linguistics: Posters* (pp. 614-622). Association for Computational Linguistics.

Mann, G. S., & Yarowsky, D. (2001). Multipath translation lexicon induction via bridge languages. *In NAACL.*

Mimno, D., Wallach, H. M., Naradowsky, J., Smith, D. A., & McCallum, A. (2009). Polylingual topic models. *In Proceedings of the 2009 Conference on Empirical Methods in Natural Language Processing: Volume 2*, (pp. 880-889).

Minkov, E., & Cohen, W. W. (2012). Graph based similarity measures for synonym extraction from parsed text. *Workshop Proceedings of TextGraphs-7 on Graph-based Methods for Natural Language Processing.* Association for Computational Linguistics.

Munteanu, D. S., & Marcu, D. (2006). Extracting parallel sub-sentential fragments from non-parallel corpora. *In Proceedings of the 21st International Conference on Computational Linguistics and the 44th annual meeting of the ACL* , (pp. 81-88).

Muthukrishnan, P., Radev, D., & Mei, Q. (2011). Simultaneous similarity learning and feature-weight learning for document clustering.". *Proceedings of textgraphs-6: Graph-based methods for natural language processing.* Association for Computational.

Neal, R. M. (2000). Markov chain sampling methods for Dirichlet process mixture models. *Journal of computational and graphical statistics, 9(2)*, 249-265.

Ni, X., Sun, J. T., Hu, J., & Chen, Z. (2009). Mining multilingual topics from wikipedia. *In Proceedings of the 18th international conference on World wide web* (pp. 1155-1156). ACM.

Och, F. J. (2003). Minimum error rate training in statistical machine translation. *Association for Computational Linguistics.* Proceedings of the

41st Annual Meeting on Association for Computational Linguistics-Volume 1.

Otero, P. G. (2007). Learning bilingual lexicons from comparable english and spanish corpora. *Proceedings of MT Summit xI*, (pp. 191-198).

Otero, P. G., & López, I. G. (2010). Wikipedia as multilingual source of comparable corpora. *In Proceedings of the 3rd Workshop on BUCC, LREC*, (pp. 21-25).

Pal, S., Pakray, P., & Naskar, S. K. (2014). Automatic Building and Using Parallel Resources for SMT from Comparable Corpora. *In Proceedings of the 3rd Workshop on Hybrid Approaches to Translation (HyTra)@ EACL*, (pp. 48-57).

Quirk, C., Udupa, R., & Menezes, A. (2007). Generative models of noisy translations with applications to parallel fragment extraction. *Proceedings of the Machine Translation Summit XI*, (pp. 377-384).

Rapp, R. (1995). Identifying word translationsin non-parallel texts. In Proceedings of Association for Computational Linguistics.

Rapp, R. (1999). Automatic identification of word translations from unrelated english and german corpora. *In Proceedings of the 37th annual meeting of the Association for Computational Linguistics on Computational Linguistics, ACL '99* (pp. 519-526). Association for Computational Linguistics.

Razmara, M., Siahbani, M., Haffari, G., & Sarkar, A. (2013). Graph propagation for paraphrasing out-of-vocabulary words in statistical machine translation. InProceedings of the Conference of the Association for Computational Linguistics (ACL).

Saluja, A., & Navrátil, J. (2013). Graph-Based Unsupervised Learning of Word Similarities Using Heterogeneous Feature Types. *Graph-Based Methods for Natural Language Processin*.

Saralegui, X. I., San Vicente, I., & Gurrutx-aga, A. (2008). Automatic generation of bilingual lexicons from comparable corpora in a popular science domain. *In LREC 2008 workshop on BUCC*.

Schafer, C., & Yarowsky, D. (2002). Iducing translation lexicons via diverse similarity measures and bridge languages. *In proceedings of the 6th conference on Natural language learning - Volume 20, COLING-02* (pp. 1-7). Stroudsburg, PA, USA: Association for Computational Linguistics.

Shezaf, D., & Rappoport, A. (2010). Bilingual lexicon generation using non-aligned signatures. *In Proceedings of the 48th annual meeting of the association for computational linguistics* (pp. 98-107). Association for Computational Linguistics.

Soderland, S., Etzioni, O., Weld, D. S., Skinner, M., & Bilmes, J. (2009). Compiling a massive, multilingual dictionary via probabilistic inference. *In Proceedings of the Joint Conference of the 47th Annual Meeting of the ACL and the 4th International Joint Conference on Natural Language Processing of the AFNLP: Volume 1*, (pp. 262-270).

Stolcke, A. (2002). SRILM-an extensible language modeling toolkit. *In INTERSPEECH*. .

Wu, H., & Wang, H. (2007). Pivot language approach for phrase-based statistical machine translation. *Machine Translation 21.3*, 165-181.

Xiang, L., Zhou, Y., & Zon, C. (2013). An Efficient Framework to Extract Parallel Units from Comparable Data. *Natural Language Processing and Chinese Computing Springer Berlin Heidelberg*, 151-163.

Evaluating Features for Identifying Japanese-Chinese Bilingual Synonymous Technical Terms from Patent Families

Zi Long
Takehito Utsuro
Grad. Sch. Sys. & Inf. Eng.,
University of Tsukuba,
Tsukuba, 305-8573, Japan

Tomoharu Mitsuhashi
Japan Patent
Information Organization,
4-1-7, Tokyo, Koto-ku,
Tokyo, 135-0016, Japan

Mikio Yamamoto
Grad. Sch. Sys. & Inf. Eng.,
University of Tsukuba,
Tsukuba, 305-8573, Japan

Abstract

In the process of translating patent documents, a bilingual lexicon of technical terms is inevitable knowledge source. It is important to develop techniques of acquiring technical term translation equivalent pairs automatically from parallel patent documents. We take an approach of utilizing the phrase table of a state-of-the-art phrase-based statistical machine translation model. First, we collect candidates of synonymous translation equivalent pairs from parallel patent sentences. Then, we apply the Support Vector Machines (SVMs) to the task of identifying bilingual synonymous technical terms. This paper especially focuses on the issue of examining the effectiveness of each feature and identifies the minimum number of features that perform as comparatively well as the optimal set of features. Finally, we achieve the performance of over 90% precision with the condition of more than or equal to 25% recall.

1 Introduction

For both high quality machine and human translation, a large scale and high quality bilingual lexicon is the most important key resource. Since manual compilation of bilingual lexicon requires plenty of time and huge manual labor, in the research area of knowledge acquisition from natural language text, automatic bilingual lexicon compilation have been studied. Techniques invented so far include translation term pair acquisition based on statistical co-occurrence measure from parallel sentences (Matsumoto and Utsuro, 2000), compositional translation generation based on an existing bilingual lexicon for human use (Tonoike et al., 2006), translation term pair acquisition by collecting partially bilingual texts through the search engine (Huang et al., 2005), and translation term pair acquisition from comparable corpora (Fung and Yee, 1998; Aker et al., 2013; Kontonatsios et al., 2014; Rapp and Sharoff, 2014).

Among those efforts of acquiring bilingual lexicon from text, Morishita et al. (2008) studied to acquire Japanese-English technical term translation lexicon from phrase tables, which are trained by a phrase-based SMT model with parallel sentences automatically extracted from parallel patent documents. Furthermore, based on the achievement above, Liang et al. (2011a) studied the issue of identifying Japanese-English synonymous translation equivalent pairs in the task of acquiring Japanese-English technical term translation equivalent pairs. Based on the technique and the results of identifying Japanese-English synonymous translation equivalent pairs in Liang et al. (2011a), Long et al. (2014) next studied how to identify Japanese-Chinese synonymous translation equivalent pairs from Japanese-Chinese patent families.

In the task of identifying Japanese-Chinese synonymous translation equivalent pairs from Japanese-Chinese patent families (Figure 1) studied in Long et al. (2014), this paper modifies some of the features studied in Long et al. (2014) and further focuses on the issue of examining the effectiveness of each feature. This paper especially identifies the minimum number of features that perform as comparatively well as the optimal set of features, where the most effective feature is discovered to be the rate of intersection in translation by the phrase table. Based on the evaluation results, we finally achieve the performance of over 90% precision with the condition of more than or equal to 25% recall.

2 Japanese-Chinese Parallel Patent Documents

Japanese-Chinese parallel patent documents are collected from the Japanese patent documents

Long Paper Proceedings of the Eighth Workshop on Building and Using Comparable Corpora, pages 52–61,
Beijing, China, July 30, 2015.

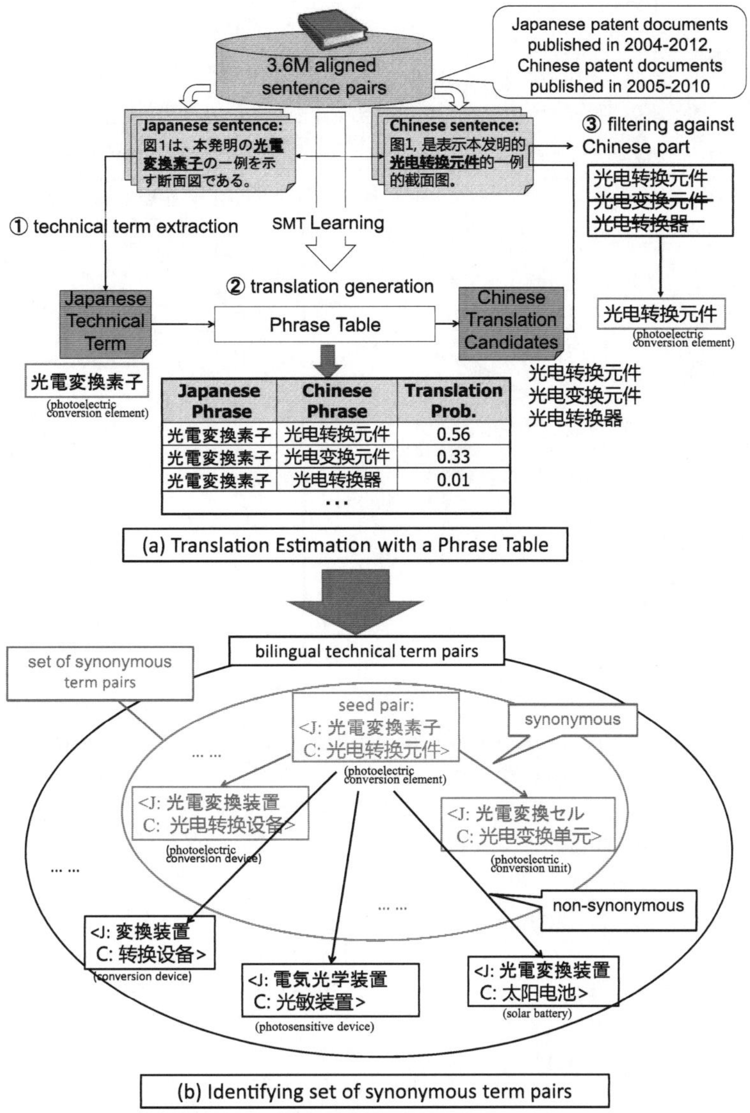

Figure 1: Framework of Identifying Japanese-Chinese Bilingual Synonymous Technical Terms from Patent Families

published by the Japanese Patent Office (JPO) in 2004-2012 and the Chinese patent documents published by State Intellectual Property Office of the People's Republic of China (SIPO) in 2005-2010. From them, we extract 312,492 patent families, and the method of Utiyama and Isahara (2007) is applied[1] to the text of those patent families, and Japanese and Chinese sentences are aligned. In this paper, we use 3.6M parallel patent sentences with the highest scores of sentence alignment[2].

[1] We used a Japanese-Chinese translation lexicon consisting of about 170,000 Chinese head words.

[2] The maximum score of the method of Utiyama and Isahara (2007) is set to be 1.0, while the lower bound of its score is about 0.152 with the 3.6M parallel patent sentences.

3 Phrase Table of an SMT Model

As a toolkit of a phrase-based SMT model, we use Moses (Koehn et al., 2007) and apply it to the whole 3.6M parallel patent sentences. Before applying Moses, Japanese sentences are segmented into a sequence of morphemes by the Japanese morphological analyzer MeCab[3] with the morpheme lexicon IPAdic[4]. For Chinese sentences, we examine two types of segmentation,

[3] http://mecab.sourceforge.net/

[4] http://sourceforge.jp/projects/ipadic/

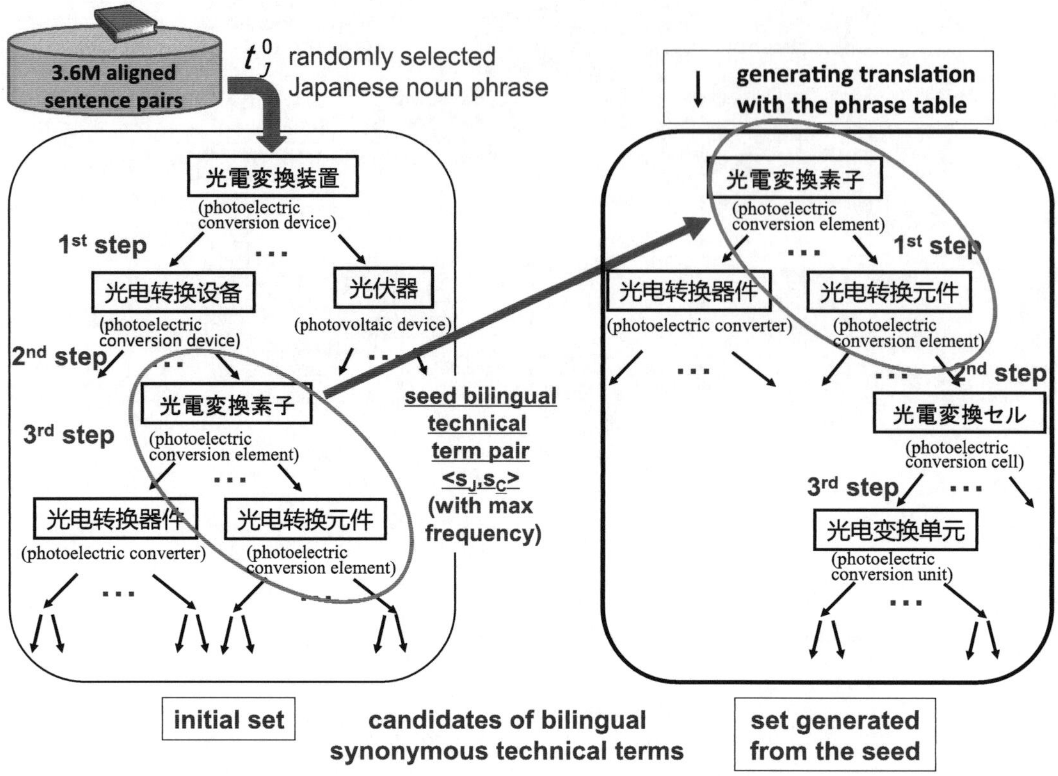

Figure 2: Developing a Reference Set of Bilingual Synonymous Technical Terms

i.e., segmentation by characters[5] and segmentation by morphemes[6].

As the result of applying Moses, we have a phrase table in the direction of Japanese to Chinese translation, and another one in the opposite direction of Chinese to Japanese translation. In the direction of Japanese to Chinese translation, when Chinese side of parallel sentences are segmented by morphemes, we finally obtain 108M translation pairs with 75M unique Japanese phrases with Japanese to Chinese phrase translation probabilities $P(p_C \mid p_J)$ of translating a Japanese phrase p_J into a Chinese phrase p_C. When Chinese sentences are segmented by characters, on the other hand, we obtain 274M translation pairs with 197M unique Japanese phrases. For each Japanese phrase, those multiple translation candidates in the phrase table are ranked in descending order of Japanese to Chinese phrase translation probabilities. In the similar way, in the phrase table in the opposite direction of Chinese to Japanese translation, for each Chinese phrase, multiple Japanese translation candidates are ranked in descending order of Chinese to Japanese phrase translation probabilities.

Those two phrase tables are then referred to when identifying a bilingual technical term pair, given a parallel sentence pair $\langle S_J, S_C \rangle$ and a Japanese technical term t_J, or a Chinese technical term t_C. In the direction of Japanese to Chinese, as shown in Figure 1 (a), given a parallel sentence pair $\langle S_J, S_C \rangle$ containing a Japanese technical term t_J, Chinese translation candidates collected from the Japanese to Chinese phrase table are matched against the Chinese sentence S_C of the parallel sentence pair. Among those found in S_C, $\hat{t}_C$ with the largest translation probability $P(t_C \mid t_J)$ is selected and the bilingual technical term pair $\langle t_J, \hat{t}_C \rangle$ is identified. Similarly, in the opposite direction of Chinese to Japanese, given a parallel sentence pair $\langle S_J, S_C \rangle$ containing a Chinese technical term t_C, the Chinese to Japanese

[5] A consecutive sequence of numbers as well as a consecutive sequence of alphabetical characters are segmented into a token.

[6] Chinese sentences are segmented into a sequence of morphemes by the Chinese morphological analyzer Stanford Word Segment (Tseng et al., 2005) trained with Chinese Penn Treebank.

phrase table is referred to when identifying a bilingual technical term pair.

4 Developing a Reference Set of Bilingual Synonymous Technical Terms

When developing a reference set of bilingual synonymous technical terms (detailed procedure to be found in Long et al. (2014)), as illustrated in Figure 2, starting from a seed bilingual term pair $s_{JC} = \langle s_J, s_C \rangle$, we repeat the translation estimation procedure of the previous section in both Japanese-Chinese direction and Chinese-Japanese direction six times in total, and generate the set $CBP(s_J)$ of candidates of bilingual synonymous technical term pairs. Then, we manually divide the set $CBP(s_J)$ into $SBP(s_{JC})$, those of which are synonymous with s_{JC}, and the remaining $NSBP(s_{JC})$. As in Table 1, we collect 114 seeds, where the number of bilingual technical terms included in $SBP(s_{JC})$ in total for all of the 114 seed bilingual technical term pairs is around 2,300 to 2,400, which amounts to around 21 per seed on average[7]. As shown in Figure 1 (b), to all of those bilingual term pairs, the procedure of identifying the synonymous sets is applied.

5 Identifying Bilingual Synonymous Technical Terms by Machine Learning

In this section, we apply the Support Vector Machines (SVMs) (Vapnik, 1998) to the task of identifying bilingual synonymous technical terms. In this paper, we model the task of identifying bilingual synonymous technical terms by the SVMs as that of judging whether or not the input bilingual term pair $\langle t_J, t_C \rangle$ is synonymous with the seed bilingual technical term pair $s_{JC} = \langle s_J, s_C \rangle$.

5.1 The Procedure

First, let CBP be the union of the sets $CBP(s_J)$ of candidates of bilingual synonymous technical term pairs for all of the 114 seed bilingual technical term pairs. In the training and testing of the classifier for identifying bilingual synonymous technical terms, we first divide the set of 114 seed bilingual technical term pairs into 10 subsets. Here, for each i-th subset ($i = 1, \ldots, 10$), we construct the union CBP_i of the sets $CBP(s_J)$ of candidates of bilingual synonymous technical term pairs, where $CBP_1, \ldots, CBP_{10}$ are 10 disjoint subsets[8] of CBP.

As a tool for learning SVMs, we use TinySVM (`http://chasen.org/~taku/software/TinySVM/`). As the kernel function, we use the polynomial (1st order) kernel[9]. In the testing of a SVMs classifier, we regard the distance from the separating hyperplane to each test instance as a confidence measure, and return test instances satisfying confidence measures over a certain lower bound only as positive samples (i.e., synonymous with the seed). In the training of SVMs, we use 8 subsets out of the whole 10 subsets $CBP_1, \ldots, CBP_{10}$. Then, we tune the lower bound of the confidence measure with one of the remaining two subsets. With this subset, we also tune the parameter of TinySVM for trade-off between training error and margin. Finally, we test the trained classifier against another one of the remaining two subsets. We repeat this procedure of training / tuning / testing 10 times, and average the 10 results of test performance.

5.2 Features

Table 2 lists all the features used for training and testing of SVMs for identifying bilingual synonymous technical terms. Features are roughly divided into two types: those of the first type $f_1, \ldots, f_6$ simply represent various characteristics of the input bilingual technical term $\langle t_J, t_C \rangle$, while those of the second type $f_7, \ldots, f_{17}$ represent relation of the input bilingual technical term $\langle t_J, t_C \rangle$ and the seed bilingual technical term pair $s_{JC} = \langle s_J, s_C \rangle$

Among the features of the first type are the frequency (f_1), ranks of terms with respect to the conditional translation probabilities (f_2 and f_3), length of terms (f_4 and f_5), and the number of times repeating the procedure of generating translation with the phrase tables until generating input terms t_J and t_C from the Japanese seed term s_J (f_6).

Among the features of the second type are identity of monolingual terms (f_7 and f_8), edit distance of monolingual terms (f_9), character bigram sim-

[7]We manually generate the reference set by discarding the bilingual pairs which are judged as not synonymous with the seed pair. The procedure of generating the whole reference sets took about 30 hours, i.e., about 3 seconds for judging a bilingual term pair on average.

[8]Here, we divide the set of 114 seed bilingual technical term pairs into 10 subsets so that the numbers of positive (i.e., synonymous with the seed) / negative (i.e., not synonymous with the seed) samples in each CBP_i ($i = 1, \ldots, 10$) are comparative among the 10 subsets.

[9]We compare the performance of the 1st order and 2nd order kernels, where we have almost comparative performance.

Table 1: Number of Bilingual Technical Terms: Candidates and Reference of Synonyms

(a) With the Phrase Table based on Chinese Sentences Segmented by Morphemes

		# of bilingual technical terms for the total 114 seeds		average per seed	
Candidates of Synonyms $\bigcup_{s_J} CBP(s_J)$	included only in the set (a)	12,640	24,621	110.9	216.0
	included in the intersection of the sets (a) and (b)	11,981		105.1	
Reference of Synonyms $\bigcup_{s_{JC}} SBP(s_{JC})$	included only in the set (a)	228	2,473	2.0	21.7
	included in the intersection of the sets (a) and (b)	2,245		19.7	

(b) With the Phrase Table based on Chinese Sentences Segmented by Characters

		# of bilingual technical terms for the total 114 seeds		average per seed	
Candidates of Synonyms $\bigcup_{s_J} CBP(s_J)$	included only in the set (b)	6,358	17,478	55.8	153.3
	included in the intersection of the sets (a) and (b)	11,120		97.5	
Reference of Synonyms $\bigcup_{s_{JC}} SBP(s_{JC})$	included only in the set (b)	287	2,318	2.5	20.3
	included in the intersection of the sets (a) and (b)	2,031		17.8	

Table 4: Pairs of Features having No Significant Difference (5% Significance Level) with Maximum Precision Features and their Evaluation Results (%)

(a) Chinese sentences are segmented by morphemes

feature	precision	recall	f-measure
$f_{15} + f_{16}$	85.6	25.4	39.2
$f_9 + f_{16}$	86.8	24.9	38.7
$f_{13} + f_{14} + f_{16}$	86.8	24.8	38.6

(b) Chinese sentences are segmented by characters

feature	precision	recall	f-measure
$f_9 + f_{15}$	87.4	25.4	39.3

ilarity of monolingual terms (f_{10}), rate of identical morphemes (in Japanese, f_{11}) / characters (in Chinese, f_{12}), string subsumption and variants for Japanese (f_{13}), identical stem for Chinese (f_{14}), rate of intersection in translation by the phrase table (f_{15}), rate of intersection in translation by the phrase table for the substrings not common between the seed and a term (f_{16}), and translation by the phrase tables (f_{17}).

As we discuss in the next section, among all of those features, f_{15} and f_{16}, which utilize the rate of intersection in translation by the phrase table, are the most effective, where we add f_{16} in this paper to those studied in Long et al. (2014).

5.3 Evaluating the Effectiveness of Features

Table 3 shows the evaluation results for a baseline as well as for SVMs. As the baseline, we simply judge the input bilingual term pair $\langle t_J, t_C \rangle$ as synonymous with the seed bilingual technical term pair $s_{JC} = \langle s_J, s_C \rangle$ when t_J and s_J are identical, or, t_C and s_C are identical. When training / testing a SVMs classifier, we tune the lower bound of the confidence measure of the distance from the separating hyperplane in two ways: i.e., for maximizing precision and for maximizing F-measure. As shown in Table 3, when we use the set of features which maximize precision, we achieve higher precisions of 89.0% and 90.4% for morpheme-based segmentation and character-based segmentation, respectively, compared with when we use all of the proposed features (86.5% and 89.0%) with the condition of more than or equal to 40% F-measure[10]. The sets of features which maximize precision are $f_{1\sim6} + f_{9\sim16}$ for morpheme-based

[10]Out of 655 (for morpheme-based segmentation) / 605 (for character-based segmentation) pairs which are correctly judged as synonymous with the seed pair by SVM , 197 (30.1%) / 161 (26.6%) are not judged as synonymous by the baseline method, i.e., neither the Japanese term nor the Chinese term is identical to that of the seed pair. On the other hand, out of 986 (for morpheme-based segmentation) / 927 (for character-based segmentation) pairs which are correctly judged as synonymous by the baseline method, 458 (46.5%) / 444 (47.9%) are judged as synonymous with the seed pair by SVM, while the rests are not judged as synonymous by SVM.

Table 2: Features for Identifying Bilingual Synonymous Technical Terms by Machine Learning

class	feature		definition (where X denotes J or C, and $\langle s_J, s_C \rangle$ denotes the seed bilingual technical term pair)
features for bilingual technical terms $\langle t_J, t_C \rangle$	f_1:	frequency	log of the frequency of $\langle t_J, t_C \rangle$ within the whole parallel patent sentences
	f_2:	rank of the Chinese term	given t_J, log of the rank of t_C with respect to the descending order of the conditional translation probability $\mathrm{P}(t_C \mid t_J)$
	f_3:	rank of the Japanese term	given t_C, log of the rank of t_J with respect to the descending order of the conditional translation probability $\mathrm{P}(t_J \mid t_C)$
	f_4:	number of Japanese characters	number of characters in t_J
	f_5:	number of Chinese characters	number of characters in t_C
	f_6:	number of times generating translation by applying the phrase tables	the number of times repeating the procedure of generating translation by applying the phrase tables until generating t_C or t_J from s_J, as in $s_C \rightarrow \cdots \rightarrow t_J \rightarrow t_C$, or, $s_J \rightarrow \cdots \rightarrow t_C \rightarrow t_J$
features for the relation of bilingual technical terms $\langle t_J, t_C \rangle$ and the seed $\langle s_J, s_C \rangle$	f_7:	identity of Japanese terms	returns 1 when $t_J = s_J$
	f_8:	identity of Chinese terms	returns 1 when $t_C = s_C$
	f_9:	edit distance similarity of monolingual terms	$f_9(t_X, s_X) = 1 - \frac{ED(t_X, s_X)}{\max(\lvert t_X \rvert, \lvert s_X \rvert)}$ (where ED is the edit distance of t_X and s_X, and $\mid t \mid$ denotes the number of characters of t.)
	f_{10}:	character bigram similarity of monolingual terms	$f_{10}(t_X, s_X) = \frac{\lvert bigram(t_X) \cap bigram(s_X) \rvert}{\max(\lvert t_X \rvert, \lvert s_X \rvert) - 1}$ (where $bigram(t)$ is the set of character bigrams of the term t.)
	f_{11}:	rate of identical morphemes (for Japanese terms)	$f_{11}(t_J, s_J) = \frac{\lvert const(t_J) \cap const(s_J) \rvert}{\max(\lvert const(t_J) \rvert, \lvert const(s_J) \rvert)}$ (where $const(t)$ is the set of morphemes in the Japanese term t.)
	f_{12}:	rate of identical characters (for Chinese terms)	$f_{11}(t_C, s_C) = \frac{\lvert const(t_C) \cap const(s_C) \rvert}{\max(\lvert const(t_C) \rvert, \lvert const(s_C) \rvert)}$ (where $const(t)$ is the set of Characters in the Chinese term t.)
	f_{13}:	subsumption relation of strings / variants relation of surface forms (for Japanese terms)	returns 1 when the difference of t_J and s_J is only in their suffixes, or only whether or not having the prolonged sound "ー", or only in their hiragana parts.
	f_{14}:	identical stem (for Chinese terms)	returns 1 when the difference of t_C and s_C is only whether or not having the word "的" which is not the prefix or suffix.
	f_{15}:	rate of intersection in translation by the phrase table	$f_{15}(t_X, s_X) = \frac{\lvert trans(t_X) \cap trans(s_X) \rvert}{\max(\lvert trans(t_X) \rvert, \lvert trans(s_X) \rvert)}$ (where $trans(t)$ is the set of translation of term t from the phrase table.)
	f_{16}:	rate of intersection in translation by the phrase table (for the substrings not common between t_X and s_X)	Suppose that $x_t^1, \ldots, x_t^m$ and $x_s^1, \ldots, x_s^n$ are the substrings which are not common between t_X and s_X. Here, we find l $(= \min(m, n))$ pairs of one-to-one mappings between x_t^i $(i = 1, \ldots, m)$ and x_s^j $(j = 1, \ldots, n)$ which maximize the product of the rates $f_{15}(x_t^i, x_s^j)$ of intersection in translation by the phrase table and return this product.
	f_{17}:	translation by the phrase table	returns 1 when s_J can be generated by translating t_C with the phrase table, or, s_C can be generated by translating t_J with the phrase table.

segmentation and $f_{2,3} + f_{6 \sim 9} + f_{11,12,15,16}$ for character-based segmentation, respectively. However, their differences are not significant (5% significance level). Next, we evaluate the effect of each single feature as well as combinations of small number of features, where, among those results, Table 4 shows pairs of features each of which achieves a precision with no significant difference (5% significance level) with the set of features having the maximum precision. It is obvious that features f_{15} and f_{16}, which utilize the rate of intersection in translation by the phrase table, are the most effective. Also, when we remove features f_{15} and f_{16} from all the features, precisions are significantly damaged (5% significance level) to 78.5% and 79.4% for morpheme-based and character-based segmentations, respectively. The reason why these features are the most effective among other features is that they directly measure the degree of being synonymous within one language with respect to the rate of intersection of translations into the other language, while other features just measure the character-based or morpheme-based similarity within one language.

We further compare the performance of the proposed features with those studied in Tsunakawa and Tsujii (2008), where we modify the features of Tsunakawa and Tsujii (2008) as shown in Table 5, and then evaluate those modified features. As we compare the performance of the proposed features and the modified features of Tsunakawa and Tsujii (2008) in Table 3, it is clear that the pro-

Table 3: Evaluation Results (%)

		segmented by morphemes			segmented by characters		
		precision	recall	f-measure	precision	recall	f-measure
baseline (t_J and s_J are identical, or, t_C and s_C are identical.)		71.4	40.0	51.3	74.0	40.1	52.0
SVM (all features)	maximum precision	**86.5**	26.5	40.5	**89.0**	26.1	40.4
	maximum f-measure	64.3	64.1	**64.2**	63.5	65.3	**64.4**
SVM (features with maximum precision)	maximum precision	**89.0**	23.9	37.7	**90.4**	25.5	40.4
		($f_{1\sim6} + f_{9\sim16}$)			($f_{2,3} + f_{6\sim9} + f_{11,12,15,16}$)		
SVM (features in Tsunakawa and Tsujii (2008))	maximum precision	72.6	26.1	38.4	74.4	36.7	49.2
	maximum f-measure	71.0	54.7	61.5	72.7	53.7	61.8

Table 5: Features for Identifying Bilingual Synonymous Technical Terms by Tsunakawa and Tsujii (2008)

class	features		definition
basical features	h_{1J}, h_{1C}:	agreement of the first characters	returns 1 when the fisrt characters of t_X and s_X match.
	h_{2J}, h_{2C}:	edit distance of similarity of monolingual terms	the same as f_9
	h_{3J}, h_{3C}:	character of bigram similarity of monolingual terms	the same as f_{10}
	h_{4J}, h_{4C}:	agreement of word substring	return the count that substrings of t_X match s_X. (Here, Tsunakawa and Tsujii (2008) count not only the common substrings but also substrings in known synonymous relation between t_X and s_X. However, in our work, we have no lexicon available for synonymous relation. So, we utilize only the count of common substrings.)
	h_{5J}, h_{5C}:	translation by the phrase table	the same as f_{17}. (Here, instead of the phrase table, Tsunakawa and Tsujii (2008) utilize a bilingual lexicon and consider the existence of bilingual lexical items as features.)
	h_6:	identical stem for Chinese terms	the same as f_{14} (Although Tsunakawa and Tsujii (2008) define this feature as examining the acronym relation of English terms, we modify this feature as examining the difference of the Chinese terms as the Chinese word "的".)
	h_7:	subsumption relation of strings / variants relation of surface forms for Japanese terms	the same as f_{13} (Although Tsunanakwa and Tsujii (2008) examine only the katakana variant, we additionally examine the difference of suffixes and variants of hiragana parts.)
combinatorial feature	$h_{1J} \wedge h_{1C}$		—
	$\sqrt{h_{2J} \cdot h_{2C}}$		—
	$\sqrt{h_{3J} \cdot h_{3C}}$		—
	$h_{5J} \wedge h_{5C}$		—
	$h_6 \cdot h_{2J}$		—
	$h_7 \cdot h_{2C}$		—

posed features outperform the modified features of Tsunakawa and Tsujii (2008).

Next, Table 6 shows examples of improvement by SVM compared with the baseline. As shown in Table 6 (a), the relation between input bilingual term pairs and seed bilingual term pairs is correctly judged as "synonym", while judgement by the baseline is "not synonym" since neither the Chinese terms nor the Japanese terms are identical. In our proposed features, f_{17} contributes to the correct judgement, where it returns 1 because of the existence of the translation pairs ⟨"ガラス転移温度","绝缘件" ⟩ and ⟨"ガラス転移点","绝热体"⟩ in the phrase table. In the case of another example shown in Table 6 (b), on the other hand, the proposed method correctly judges as "not synonym" by SVM compared with the baseline, where both the edit distance similarity

Table 6: Examples of Improvement in Identifying Bilingual Synonymous Technical Terms by SVM

Baseline:	Judge the input bilingual term pair $\langle t_J, t_C \rangle$ as synonymous with the seed bilingual term pair $\langle s_J, s_C \rangle$ when t_J and s_J are identical, or, t_C and s_C are identical.
SVM:	Maximize precision by tuning the lower bound of the confidence measure of the distance from the separating hyperplane (Chinese sentences are segmented by morphemes).

(a) Correct Judgement as "Synonym" only by SVM

seed $<s_J, s_C>$	bilingual term pair $<t_J, t_C>$	reference judgement	judgement by baseline	judgement by SVM
<グラス転移温度, 玻璃化转变温度> (glass transition temperature)	<グラス転移点, 玻璃态转化温度> (glass transition temperature)	synonym	not synonym	synonym

(b) Correct Judgement as "Not Synonym" only by SVM

seed $<s_J, s_C>$	bilingual term pair $<t_J, t_C>$	reference judgement	judgement by baseline	judgement by SVM
<集電装置, 集电器> (current collector)	<コレクト(collector), 集电器(current collector)>	not synonym	synonym	not synonym

(f_9) and the character bigram similarity (f_{10}) between the Japanese terms "集電装置" and "コレクト" are 0 ($f_9(\langle t_J, t_C \rangle, \langle s_J, s_C \rangle) = 0$ and $f_{10}(\langle t_J, t_C \rangle, \langle s_J, s_C \rangle) = 0$).

Finally, Table 7 shows examples of erroneous judgements by SVM. As shown in Table 7 (a), since erroneous translation pairs ⟨"断熱体","绝缘件"⟩ and ⟨"インシュレーター","绝热体"⟩ exist in the phrase table, both f_{17} (both of the translations pairs $\langle s_J, t_C \rangle$ and $\langle t_J, s_C \rangle$ exist in the phrase table) and f_{17} (either the translation pair $\langle s_J, t_C \rangle$ or $\langle t_J, s_C \rangle$ exist in the phrase table) return 1, resulting in erroneous judgement.

Another example is shown in Table 7 (b), where the proposed method returns erroneous judgement as "not synonym". In this case, since the translation pair ⟨"成膜チャンバー","成膜室"⟩ only exists in the phrase table, f_{17} (either the translation pair $\langle s_J, t_C \rangle$ or $\langle t_J, s_C \rangle$ exist in the phrase table) returns 1, while f_{17} (both of translations pairs $\langle s_J, t_C \rangle$ and $\langle t_J, s_C \rangle$ exist in the phrase table) returns 0. Furthermore, even though Chinese words "成膜" and "膜成形" are synonymous, their character bigram similarity is computed as 0, since they have opposite character orderings.

6 Related Work

Among related works on acquiring bilingual lexicon from text, Lu and Tsou (2009) and Yasuda and Sumita (2013) studied to extract bilingual terms from comparable patents, where, they first extract parallel sentences from comparable patents, and then extract bilingual terms from parallel sentences. Those studies differ from this paper in that those studies did not address the issue of acquiring bilingual synonymous technical terms. Tsunakawa and Tsujii (2008) is mostly related to our study, in that they also proposed to apply machine learning technique to the task of identifying bilingual synonymous technical terms. However, Tsunakawa and Tsujii (2008) studied the issue of identifying bilingual synonymous technical terms only within manually compiled bilingual technical term lexicon and thus are quite limited in its applicability. Our approach, on the other hand, is quite advantageous in that we start from parallel patent documents which continue to be published every year and then, that we can generate candidates of bilingual synonymous technical terms automatically. Furthermore, as we show in the previous section, the features proposed in this paper outperform that of Tsunakawa and Tsujii (2008).

7 Conclusion

In the task of acquiring Japanese-Chinese technical term translation equivalent pairs from parallel patent documents, this paper studied the issue of identifying synonymous translation equivalent pairs. This paper especially focused on the issue of examining the effectiveness of each feature and identified the minimum number of features that perform as comparatively well as the optimal set of features. One of the most important future work is definitely to improve recall. To do this, we plan to apply the semi-automatic framework (Liang et al., 2011b) which have been invented in the task of identifying Japanese-English synonymous translation equivalent pairs and have been proven to be effective in improving recall. Another important future work is to train the SVM of identifying bilingual synonymous technical pairs with a set

Table 7: Examples of Errors in Identifying Bilingual Synonymous Technical Terms By the Proposed Method

(a) Incorrect Judgement as "Synonym" by SVM

seed $<s_J, s_C>$	bilingual term pair $<t_J, t_C>$	for Japanese		for Chinese		feature f_{17} (by translating with the phrase table, both s_J and s_C can be generated from t_C and t_J, respectively)	feature f_{17} (by translating with the phrase table, s_J or s_C can be generated from t_C or t_J, respectively)	reference judgement	judgement by SVM
		feature f_9	feature f_{10}	feature f_9	feature f_{10}				
<断熱体 , 绝热体> (heat insulator)	<インシュレータ, 绝缘件> (insulator)	0	0	0.33	0	1	1	not synonym	synonym

(a) Incorrect Judgement as "Not Synonym" by SVM

seed $<s_J, s_C>$	bilingual term pair $<t_J, t_C>$	for Japanese		for Chinese		feature f_{17} (by translating with the phrase table, both s_J and s_C can be generated from t_C and t_J, respectively)	feature f_{17} (by translating with the phrase table, s_J or s_C can be generated from t_C or t_J, respectively)	reference judgement	judgement by SVM
		feature f_9	feature f_{10}	feature f_9	feature f_{10}				
<成膜室 , 成膜室> (film desposition chamber)	<成膜チャンバー, 膜成形室> (film desposition chamber)	0.29	0.17	0.5	0	0	1	synonym	not synonym

of patent families, and then to evaluate the trained SVM against parallel patent sentences and phrase tables extracted from another set of patent families.

References

A. Aker, M. Paramita, and R. Gaizauskas. 2013. Extracting bilingual terminologies from comparable corpora. In *Proc. 51st ACL*, pages 402–411.

P. Fung and L. Y. Yee. 1998. An IR approach for translating new words from nonparallel, comparable texts. In *Proc. 17th COLING and 36th ACL*, pages 414–420.

F. Huang, Y. Zhang, and S. Vogel. 2005. Mining key phrase translations from Web corpora. In *Proc. HLT/EMNLP*, pages 483–490.

P. Koehn, H. Hoang, A. Birch, C. Callison-Burch, M. Federico, N. Bertoldi, B. Cowan, W. Shen, C. Moran, R. Zens, C. Dyer, O. Bojar, A. Constantin, and E. Herbst. 2007. Moses: Open source toolkit for statistical machine translation. In *Proc. 45th ACL, Companion Volume*, pages 177–180.

G. Kontonatsios, I. Korkontzelos, J. Tsujii, and S. Ananiadou. 2014. Using random forest classifier to compile bilingual dictionaries of technical terms from comparable corpora. In *Proc. 14th EACL*, pages 111–116.

B. Liang, T. Utsuro, and M. Yamamoto. 2011a. Identifying bilingual synonymous technical terms from phrase tables and parallel patent sentences. *Procedia - Social and Behavioral Sciences*, 27:50–60.

B. Liang, T. Utsuro, and M. Yamamoto. 2011b. Semi-automatic identification of bilingual synonymous technical terms from phrase tables and parallel patent sentences. In *Proc. 25th PACLIC*, pages 196–205.

Z. Long, L. Dong, T. Utsuro, T. Mitsuhashi, and M. Yamamoto. 2014. Identifying Japanese-Chinese bilingual synonymous technical terms from patent families. In *Proc. 7th BUCC*, pages 49–54.

B. Lu and B. K. Tsou. 2009. Towards bilingual term extraction in comparable patents. In *Proc. 23rd PACLIC*, pages 755–762.

Y. Matsumoto and T. Utsuro. 2000. Lexical knowledge acquisition. In R. Dale, H. Moisl, and H. Somers, editors, *Handbook of Natural Language Processing*, chapter 24, pages 563–610. Marcel Dekker Inc.

Y. Morishita, T. Utsuro, and M. Yamamoto. 2008. Integrating a phrase-based SMT model and a bilingual lexicon for human in semi-automatic acquisition of technical term translation lexicon. In *Proc. 8th AMTA*, pages 153–162.

R. Rapp and S. Sharoff. 2014. Extracting multiword translations from aligned comparable documents. In *Proc. 3rd Workshop on Hybrid Approaches to Translation*, pages 83–91.

M. Tonoike, M. Kida, T. Takagi, Y. Sasaki, T. Utsuro, and S. Sato. 2006. A comparative study on compositional translation estimation using a domain/topic-specific corpus collected from the web. In *Proc. 2nd Intl. Workshop on Web as Corpus*, pages 11–18.

H. Tseng, P. Chang, G. Andrew, D. Jurafsky, and C. Manning. 2005. A conditional random field word segmenter for Sighan bakeoff 2005. In *Proc. 4th SIGHAN Workshop on Chinese Language Processing*, pages 168–171.

T. Tsunakawa and J. Tsujii. 2008. Bilingual synonym identification with spelling variations. In *Proc. 3rd IJCNLP*, pages 457–464.

M. Utiyama and H. Isahara. 2007. A Japanese-English patent parallel corpus. In *Proc. MT Summit XI*, pages 475–482.

V. N. Vapnik. 1998. *Statistical Learning Theory*. Wiley-Interscience.

K. Yasuda and E. Sumita. 2013. Building a bilingual dictionary from a Japanese-Chinese patent corpus. In *Computational Linguistics and Intelligent Text Processing*, volume 7817 of *LNCS*, pages 276–284. Springer.

Extracting Bilingual Lexica from Comparable Corpora Using Self-Organizing Maps

Hyeong-Won Seo **Min-Ah Cheon** **Jae-Hoon Kim**

Department of Computer Engineering, Korea Maritime and Ocean University,
Busan 606-791, Republic of Korea

wonn24@gmail.com minah014@outlook.com jhoon@kmou.ac.kr

Abstract

This paper aims to present a novel method of extracting bilingual lexica from comparable corpora using one of the artificial neural network algorithms, self-organizing maps (SOMs). The proposed method is very useful when a seed dictionary for translating source words into target words is insufficient. Our experiments have shown stunning results when contrasted with one of the other approaches. For future work, we need to fine-tune various parameters to achieve stronger performances. Also we should investigate how to construct good synonym vectors.

1 Introduction

Bilingual lexicon extraction from comparable corpora has been studied by many researchers since the late 1990s (Fung, 1998; Rapp 1999; Chiao & Zweigenbaum, 2002; Ismail & Manandhar, 2010; Hazem & Morin, 2012).

To our knowledge, one of the basic approaches is the context vector-based approach (Rapp, 1995; Fung, 1998) called the standard approach in the literatures, and many other studies have been derived from this approach. Some of these are concerned with similarity score measurement (Fung, 1998; Rapp, 1999; Koehn & Knight, 2002; Prochasson *et al.*, 2009), the size of the context window (Daille & Morin, 2005; Prochasson *et al.*, 2009), and the size of the seed dictionary (Fung, 1998; Rapp, 1999; Chiao & Zweigenbaum, 2002; Koehn & Knight, 2002; Daille & Morin, 2005). The extended approach, one of such approaches, (Déjean *et al.*, 2002; Daille & Morin, 2005) has been proposed in order to reduce the load on the seed dictionary. It gathers k nearest neighbors to augment the context of the word to be translated. In spite of their efforts, using comparable corpora for extracting such lexica yields quite poor performances unless orthographic features are used. However, such features may bring other costs.

Under the circumstances like this, this paper is motivated to propose an efficient method in which comparable corpora with a minimum of resources are considered for extracting bilingual lexica. The SOM-based approach, we propose in this paper, can yield stronger performances with the same experimental circumstance than earlier studies can do. In order to show this, we compare the proposed method to the standard approach. Of course, it does not meaning our method outperforms for every data. We just show the proposed method is reasonable for this field.

The rest of the paper is structured as follows: Section 2 presents several works closely related to our method. Section 3 describes our method (the SOM-based approach) in more detail. Section 4 shows experimental results with discussions, and Section 5 concludes the paper and presents future research directions.

2 Related Works

2.1 Context-based approach

As has been noted earlier, the standard approach (Rapp, 1995; Fung, 1998) is proposed to extract bilingual lexica from comparable corpora. It uses

Short Paper Proceedings of the Eighth Workshop on Building and Using Comparable Corpora, pages 62–67,
Beijing, China, July 30, 2015. ©2015 Association for Computational Linguistics

contextually relevant words in a small-sized window. Selecting similar context vectors between source and target languages is the key feature of the approach. Since the approach uses comparable corpora, a seed dictionary to translate one to another language is required. Additionally, a large scale of corpora as well as sufficient amount of initial seed dictionaries should be prepared for a better performance.

2.2 Self-organizing maps

A self-organizing map (SOM) (Kohonen, 1982; 1995) is one of the artificial neural network models and represents a huge amount of input data in a more illustrative form in a lower-dimensional space. In general, a SOM is an unsupervised and competitive learning network. It has been studied extensively in recent years. For example, SOMs have been studied in pattern recognition (Li *et al.*, 2006; Ghorpade *et al.*, 2010), signal processing (Wakuya *et al.*, 2007), multivariate statistical analysis (Nag *et al.*, 2005), data mining (Júnior *et al.*, 2013), word categorization (Klami & Lagus, 2006), and clustering (Juntunen *et al.*, 2013).

Since a SOM tries to keep the topological properties of input data, semantically/geometrically similar inputs are generally mapped around one neuron, usually in the form of a two-dimensional lattice (*i.e.* a map). Significantly, the SOM can be used for clustering the input vectors and finding features inherent to the problem. In this perspective, we can expect that actual similar words have one common winner (winning neuron) or share the same neighbors if input vectors are semantically well-formed.

Based on this characteristic, a main idea of the proposed method is to make two different words that are translations of each other have one common winner. If a new input data has a similar input trained already, the SOMs can extract its translations based on its neighbors. Consequently, neighbors (i.e. semantically similar words) also share similar areas in the feature map.

3 SOM-based approach

The overall structure of the SOM-based approach can be summarized as follows (see Figure 1 for more details):

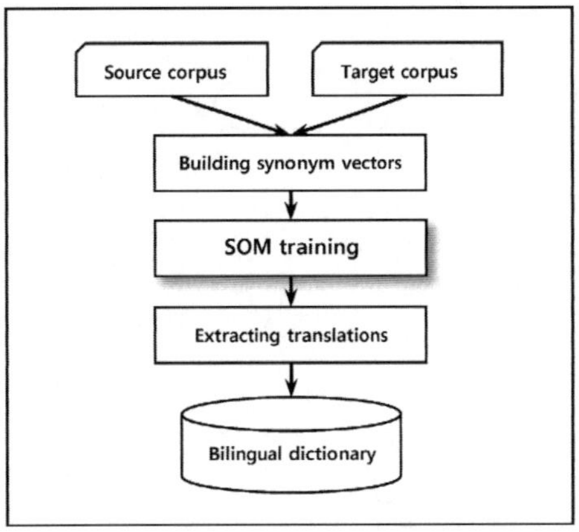

Figure 1. Overall structure of SOM-based approach

i. Building synonym vectors: In this paper, the synonym vector indicates a vector that consists of words semantically related to each other. Therefore, synonym vectors should be constructed in a semantic fashion not a co-relational fashion. For example, the vector for *baby* should very similar to the vector for *kid* not just for closely related *toy* or *sitter*. Therefore, building synonym vectors is one of the most important issues in this work. For this, we firstly build context vectors via contextually related words in a fixed-size window. This context vector is weighted by an association measure, such as the PMI or the chi-square. After context vectors are built, similarity scores between the vectors are computed. In this paper, the similarity score, as occurs so often in information retrieval, is computed by cosine similarity.

Synonyms can be identified based on the scores higher than a reasonable threshold. Synonym vectors are then weighted by the scores. For instance, let kid be a base word to be vectored. In this case, its elements are similarity scores between kid and the most similar k words, such as *baby*, *teenager*, and *youth*. Consequently, well-made synonym vectors have a SOM reflects the topological properties of input data and will obtain common winners after the SOMs are trained.

Note that such context vectors are very sensitive to experimental data and parameters such as association/similarity measures, so any kind of vector is welcomed here. We just assume semantically formed synonym vectors are already available before we train SOMs.

ii. SOM training: After the source and target synonym vectors are built, we train two sorts of SOMs in different ways. Figure 2 describes how two SOMs are trained interactively.

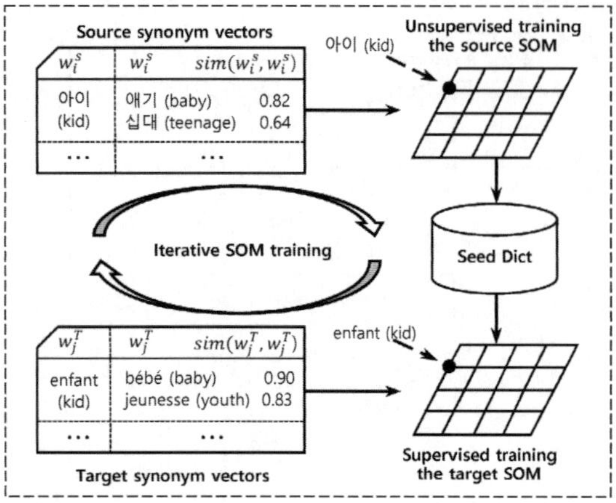

Figure 2. SOM training

Firstly, we train the source SOM in an unsupervised fashion. The general SOM algorithm to train all source words can be summarized as follows:

1) Set an initial weight vector $w(0)$ with small random values [0, 1], and set learning rate $\eta(t)$ with a small positive value ($0 < \eta(t) \leq \eta(t-1) \leq 1$). The iteration t is for one input data.

2) For every single input x, find the winning neuron (*i.e.* winner) c which has minimum score based on Euclidean distances between an input and weight vectors $\|x - w_c\| = \min_i \|x - w_i\|$.

3) Update the weight vectors of winning neuron c and its neighbors as follows:

$$w_i(t+1) = w_i(t) + \eta(t)h(t)[x(t) - w_i(t)],$$

where t denotes time, $x(t)$ is an input vector at t, and $h(t)$ is the neighborhood kernel around the winner c. In this step, we update them in online mode which means one update per one input (*c.f.* an offline mode means one update per all inputs).

4) Repeat the steps 2) and 3) until a certain termination condition like the maximum number of iterations is reached.

After the source SOM is trained in an unsupervised fashion, we train the target SOM in a supervised fashion. In this case, most of steps are the same with the case of the source. Note that we should aware of updating the target weight vectors. Target winners which of words excluded in the seed dictionary are updated naturally as the case of the source. The others which of words included in the seed dictionary are updated by calling related source winners. Therefore, two different words which are translations to each other can be located in the same topological location of two different SOMs. We think that we can teach correct labels to insiders (*i.e.* the target words that included in the seed dictionary) not for outsiders. As mentioned before, if synonym vectors are well-formed as well as two SOMs are well-trained, a source word and its translation will have one common winner. Although a target word is not trained yet, the word can be extracted when its synonym is trained.

iii. Extracting translations: After two SOMs are trained interactively, SOM vectors should be constructed based on each feature map (*i.e.* the source and target). In this case, similarity scores between an input vector and weight vectors become elements of SOM vectors. That is, a length of the SOM is a dimension of the SOM vector.

After the SOM vectors are built, similarity scores between one source SOM vector and all target SOM vectors are calculated by cosine similarity. And then, the top *k* candidates are selected and added to the bilingual lexicon.

4 Experiments

In this paper, we evaluate the proposed method for two language pairs – Korean–French (KR–FR) and Korean–Spanish (KR–ES). Regarding the comparison, we implemented the standard approach mentioned in Section 2.1. Note that the standard approach implemented here is not complete. There are many chances to show better performances by fine-tuning several parameters, such as the size of the context window, and association/similarity measures. However, we can briefly estimate them because both methods are implemented by using same resources. Several parameters are fixed as follows: the context size of the window as 5, and the association measure as a chi-square test, and the similarity measure as a cosine similarity. These measures were empirically chosen from our experimental data.

We used three comparable corpora (Kwon *et al.*, 2014) in Korean, French, and Spanish. Each corpus included around 800k sentences collected from the Web[1]. The Korean corpus consists of news articles and some are derived from different sources (Seo *et al.*, 2006). The others also consists

[1] Korean: http://www.naver.com,
French: http://www.lemonde.fr, and Spanish: http://www.abc.es

of news articles (around 400k sentences), and some are combined with the European parliament proceedings (400k randomly sampled sentences) (Koehn, 2005). The Korean corpus has around 280k word types (180k for French and 185k for Spanish), and the average number of words per sentence is 16.2 (15.9 for French and 16.1 for Spanish). Consequently, the balance of three corpora is well-formed.

We extracted nouns from these corpora for our test sets as well as input data. We considered only nouns to reduce the sizes of the dimensions of either synonym vectors or SOMs. Thus, we finally collected almost 190k Korean noun types (45k for French and 58k for Spanish). The reason why the number of Korean noun types was higher than others was due to Korean characteristics. We should split the Korean words into morpheme units because there are a lot of compound words and omitted morphemes. Furthermore, we collected very finely segmented Korean nouns to eliminate indulgent compound nouns that were possibly missed during a word segmentation task. All collected nouns were considered candidates of both test sets and seed words independently.

After the input data was prepared, we built synonym vectors, as mentioned previously. We already introduced the method how to construct synonym vectors. However, this paper doesn't mainly propose the efficient way of representing words semantically in vector spaces. If synonym vectors are built based on context vectors and their similarity scores, the size of the vector dimension would be very huge. It would cause many time-consuming problems. In this paper, we simply use word2vec[2] to build synonym vectors. As far as we know, word2vec cannot yield semantically related vectors as output. However, we used this tool to reduce vector sizes and assume these outputs (*i.e.* vectors) are reasonable as the input data for training SOMs. Some parameters for building synonym vectors can be presented as follows: window size is 5, word vector size is 100, and training iteration is 100.

4.1 Evaluation dictionary

We manually built evaluation dictionaries to evaluate our method because such dictionaries for KR–FR/–ES are publicly unavailable. Each dictionary contains 200 high-frequency nouns. The reason why we picked high-frequency nouns is that these nouns have more chances to have neighbors than low-frequency words. In order to evaluate whether the proposed approach is valid (*i.e.* whether trained SOM can extract new input data that not trained), we need to train words having many neighbors. These 200 source words were selected if actual translations were in their corpora. Thus, the 200th source word did not indicate a 200th high-frequency word. The KR→FR[3] dictionary had total of 288 translations (451 translations in the FR→KR dictionary), and the KR→ES dictionary contained 377 translations (687 translations in the ES→KR dictionary). Additionally, regretfully, there were several duplicated translations for every language. In the case of KR–FR, the Korean words had 447 French translations (420 types) and the French words had 209 Korean translations (189 types). In the case of KR–ES, the Korean words had 456 Spanish translations (369 types) and the Spanish words had 509 Korean translations (421 types). We did not perform any heuristic process to give each source word a unique sense. Instead, we assumed related source words corresponding to a single translation were semantically the same.

4.2 Seed dictionary

The seed dictionaries were also built manually based on the high-frequency nouns as mentioned before. Seed words, however, were not overlapped with evaluation data. We chose 11,910 Korean noun types (8,105 French types and 7,458 Spanish types) out of 94% of the total words in the corpus. As mentioned before, 11,910 Korean noun types out of 190k (total) noun types is an extremely low number. Except 200 of the highest-frequency words (contained in the evaluation dictionary), we finally collected 2,399 Korean seed nouns having their translations in the target corpora for KR→FR, 4,387 Korean seed nouns for KR→ES, 2,138 French seed nouns for FR→KR, and 1,813 Spanish seed nouns for ES→KR, respectively.

5 Results

Unfortunately, we do not have a publicly accepted gold standard or experimental guidelines in these language pairs. By and large, the best performances depended on various experimental settings, such as languages, document domains, and

[2] http://code.google.com/p/word2vec/

[3] The symbol '→' means unidirectional way (*i.e.* source to target only).

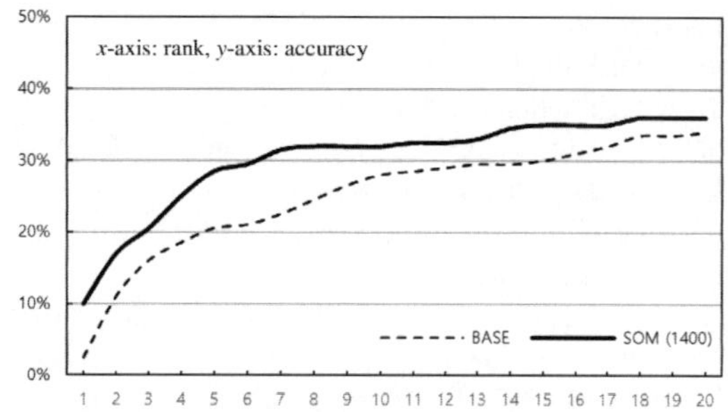

Figure 2. Accuracies of the KR→FR pair

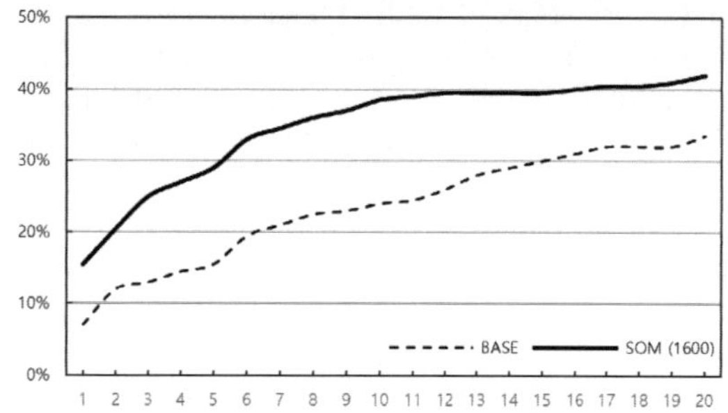

Figure 3. Accuracies of the FR→KR pair

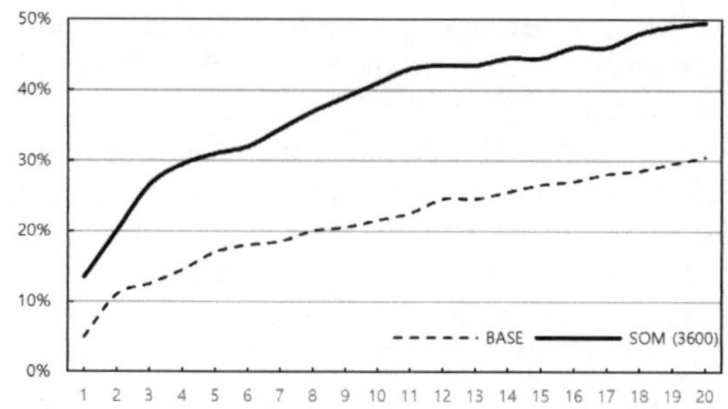

Figure 4. Accuracies of the KR→ES pair

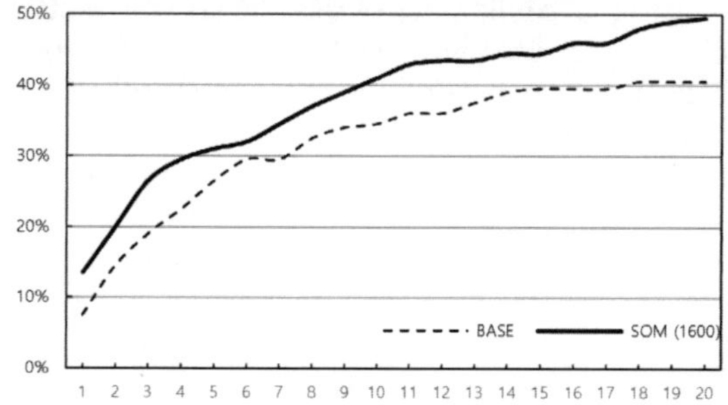

Figure 5. Accuracies of the ES→KR pair

seed dictionaries. Doubtless, the quality of synonym vectors and seed dictionaries including trained SOMs are the most important issues for achieving high performances. Additionally, we ignore evaluations of the quality of synonym vectors in this paper. We only consider accuracies for the top 20 candidates for two sets of language pairs (*i.e.* KR–FR and KR–ES).

For simplified experiments, we fixed several parameters as follows: The dimension of the synonym vector as 100, the size of the Gaussian function as 25 (5×5), the learning rate as 0.1, and the epoch as 2000. These parameters were given based on preceding experiments. In case of a SOM size, all sizes are different for covering most of seed words (one-to-one mapping had shown poor performances due to the fixed and small-sized Gaussian function). We tried to find the best parameters via fine-tuning, but most could be further improved in future research.

The accuracies for two sets of language pairs are described in Figures 2 to 5. In those figures, the BASE means the standard approach, the SOM means the SOM-based approach, the number around brackets means a size of the SOM, *x*-axis indicates ranks, and *y*-axis indicates accuracies. As can be seen, the SOM-based approach outperformed the standard approach over all language settings.

In our experimental results of the KR to FR pair, for example, we extracted *stratégie* (strategy) as the translation of the source word 전략 (jeonryak[4]; strategy, operation) where their neighbors, 작전 [5] (jakjeon; operation, tactic, strategy) and *opération*[6] (operation), are included in the seed dictionary. If new input data (to be tested) have very similar seed words, we can extract correct translations through well-trained SOMs. Although the sizes of SOMs were neither the same nor the best sizes, we can see the proposed approach is quite outstanding compared with the standard approach.

6 Conclusion

This paper proposes a novel method for extracting bilingual lexica from comparable corpora by using SOMs. The method trains two sorts of SOMs, either in an unsupervised fashion and a supervised fashion, respectively. As we can see the experimental results, our method generally outperforms the standard approach under the same experimental conditions (*i.e.* the same seed dictionaries and corpora). Although the given parameters are not the best for both approaches so far, our method shows stunning results.

For future work, we can tune parameter factors such as the size of SOMs, the Gaussian function, and the epoch. Moreover, various parts-of-speech

[4] The Korean gloss is presented before a semicolon in brackets.

[5] The similarity score between 작전 and 전략 is 0.88.

[6] The similarity score between opération and stratégie is 0.82.

could be considered, as we only considered nouns in this work. In addition, a deep analysis of errors is required.

Acknowledgements

This work was supported by the ICT R&D program of MSIP/IITP. [10041807 , Development of Original Software Technology for Automatic Speech Translation with Performance 90% for Tour/International Event focused on Multilingual Expansibility and based on Knowledge Learning]

References

Y.-C. Chiao and P. Zweigenbaum. 2002. Looking for candidate translational equivalents in specialized, comparable corpora. In *Proceedings of the 19th international conference on Computational Linguistics*, Coling'02, pp. 1208–1212.

B. Daille and E. Morin. 2005. French-English terminology extraction from comparable corpora. In *Proceedings of the 2nd International Joint Conference on Natural Language Processing*, IJCNLP'05, pp. 707–718.

H. Déjean, É. Gaussier, and F. Sadat. 2002. An approach based on multilingual thesauri and model combination for bilingual lexicon extraction. In *Proceedings of the 19th International Conference on Computational Linguistics (COLING'02)*, 1: 1-7.

P. Fung. 1998. A statistical view on bilingual lexicon extraction: from parallel corpora to non-parallel corpora. In *Proceedings of the 3rd conference of the Association for Machine Translation in the Americas*, Amta'98, pp. 1–16.

S. Ghorpade, J. Ghorpade, and S. Mantri. 2010. Pattern Recognition Using Neural Networks. *International Journal of Computer Science & Information Technology*, IJCSIT, 2(6): 92-98.

A. Hazem and E. Morin. 2012. Qalign: A new method for bilingual lexicon extraction from comparable corpora. In *Proceedings of the 13th International Conference on Computational Linguistics and Intelligent Text Processing*, CICLing'12, volume 2 of Lecture Notes in Computer Science, pp. 83–96.

A. Ismail and S. Manandhar. 2010. Bilingual lexicon extraction from comparable corpora using in-domain terms. In *Proceedings of the 23rd International Conference on Computational Linguistics*, Coling'10, pp. 481–489.

E. Júnior, G. Breda, E. Marques, and L. Mendes. 2013. Knowledge discovery: Data mining by self-organizing maps. *Web Information Systems and Technologies*, Lecture Notes in Business Information Processing, 140: 185–200.

P. Juntunen, M. Liukkonen, M. Lehtola, and H. Yrjö. 2013. Cluster analysis by self-organizing maps: An application to the modelling of water quality in a treatment process. *Applied Soft Computing*, 13(7): 3191–3196.

M. Klami and K. Lagus. 2006. Unsupervised word categorization using self-organizing maps and automatically extracted morphs. *Intelligent Data Engineering and Automated Learning*, IDEAL 2006, volume 4224 of Lecture Notes in Computer Science, pp. 912–919.

P. Koehn and K. Knight. 2002. Learning a translation lexicon from monolingual corpora, In *Proceedings of the Association for computational linguistic on unsupervised lexical acquisition*, pp. 9–16.

P. Koehn. 2005. Europarl: a parallel corpus for statistical machine translation. In *Proceeding of 10th Conference on Machine Translation Summit*, 79–86.

T. Kohonen. 1982. Self-organized formation of topologically correct feature maps. In *Biological Cybernetics*, 43(1): 59–69.

T. Kohonen. 1995. Self-organizing maps. Springer, volume 30.

H. Kwon, H.-W. Seo, M.-A. Cheon, and J.-H. Kim. 2014. Iterative bilingual lexicon extraction from comparable corpora using a modified perceptron algorithm. *Journal of Contemporary Engineering Sciences*, 7(24): 1335–1343.

C. Li, H. Zhang, J. Wang, and R. Zhao. 2006. A new pattern recognition model based on heuristic SOM network and rough set theory. In *Vehicular Electronics and Safety 2006*, ICVES 2006, IEEE International Conference on, pp. 45–48.

A. K. Nag, A. Mitra, and S. Mitra. 2005. Multiple outlier detection in multivariate data using self-organizing maps title. *Computational Statistics*, 20(2): 245–264.

E. Prochasson, E. Morin, and K. Kageura. 2009. Anchor points for bilingual lexicon extraction from small comparable corpora. In *Proceedings of the 12th Conference on Machine Translation Summit (MT Summit XII)*, pp. 284–291.

R. Rapp. 1995. Identifying word translations in non-parallel texts. In *Proceedings of the Annual Meeting of the Association for Computational Linguistics*, ACL '33, pp. 320–322.

R. Rapp. 1999. Automatic identification of word translations from unrelated English and German corpora. In *Proceedings of the 37th Annual Meeting of the Association for Computational Linguistics*, ACL '99, pp. 519–526.

H.-W. Seo, H.-C. Kim, H.-Y. Cho, J.-H. Kim, and S.-I. Yang. 2006. Automatically constructing English–Korean parallel corpus from Web documents (in Korean). In *Proceeding of 26th Conference on Korea Information Processing Society fall conference*, KIPS, 13(2): 161–164.

H. Wakuya, H. Harada, and K. Shida. 2007. An architecture of self-organizing map for temporal signal processing and its application to a braille recognition task (in Japanese). *Systems and Computers in Japan*, 38(3):62–71. Translated from Denshi Joho Tsushin Gakkai Ronbunshi, J87-D-II (3): 884–892.

Obtaining SMT dictionaries for related languages

Miguel Rios, Serge Sharoff
Centre for Translation Studies
University of Leeds
m.riosgaona,s.sharoff@leeds.ac.uk

Abstract

This study explores methods for developing Machine Translation dictionaries on the basis of word frequency lists coming from comparable corpora. We investigate (1) various methods to measure the similarity of cognates between related languages, (2) detection and removal of noisy cognate translations using SVM ranking. We show preliminary results on several Romance and Slavonic languages.

1 Introduction

Cognates are words having similarities in their spelling and meaning in two languages, either because the two languages are typologically related, e.g., *maladie* vs *malattia* ('disease'), or because they were both borrowed from the same source (*informatique* vs *informatica*). The advantage of their use in Statistical Machine Translation (SMT) is that the procedure can be based on comparable corpora, i.e., similar corpora which are not translations of each other (Sharoff et al., 2013). Given that there are more sources of comparable corpora in comparison to parallel ones, the lexicon obtained from them is likely to be richer and more variable.

Detection of cognates is a well-known task, which has been explored for a range of languages using different methods. The two main approaches applied to detection of the cognates are the generative and discriminative paradigms. The first one is based on detection of the edit distance between potential candidate pairs. The distance can be a simple Levenshtein distance, or a distance measure with the scores learned from an existing parallel set (Tiedemann, 1999; Mann and Yarowsky, 2001). The discriminative paradigm uses standard approaches to machine learning, which are based on (1) extracting features, e.g., character n-grams, and (2) learning to predict the transformations of the source word needed to (Jiampojamarn et al., 2010; Frunza and Inkpen, 2009). Given that SMT is usually based on a full-form lexicon, one of the possible issues in generation of cognates concerns the similarity of words in their root form vs the similarity in endings. For example, the Ukrainian wordform ближнього 'near$_{gen}$' is cognate to Russian ближнего, the root is identical, while the ending is considerably different (ього vs его). Regular differences in the endings, which are shared across a large number of words, can be learned separately from the regular differences in the roots.

One also needs to take into account the false friends among cognates. For example, *diseñar* means 'to design' in Spanish vs *desenhar* in Portuguese means 'to draw'. There are also often cases of partial cognates, when the words share the meaning in some contexts, but not in others, e.g., жена in Russian means 'wife', while its Bulgarian cognate жена has two meanings: 'wife' and 'woman'. Yet another complexity concerns a frequency mismatch. Two cognates might differ in their frequency. For example, *dibujo* in Spanish ('a drawing', rank 1779 in the Wikipedia frequency list) corresponds to a relatively rare cognate word *debuxo* in Portuguese (rank 104,514 in Wikipedia), while another Portuguese word *desenho* is more commonly used in this sense (rank 884 in the Portuguese Wikipedia). For MT tasks we need translations that are equally appropriate in the source and target language, therefore cognates useful for a high-quality dictionary for SMT need to have roughly the same frequency in comparable corpora and they need to be used in similar contexts.

This study investigates the settings for extracting cognates for related languages in Romance and Slavonic language families for the task of reducing the number of unknown words for SMT. This in-

Short Paper Proceedings of the Eighth Workshop on Building and Using Comparable Corpora, pages 68–73,
Beijing, China, July 30, 2015. ©2015 Association for Computational Linguistics

cludes the effects of having constraints for the cognates to be similar in their roots and in the endings, to occur in distributionally similar contexts and to have similar frequency.

2 Methodology

The methodology for producing the list of cognates is based on the following steps: 1) Produce several lists of cognates using a family of distance measures, discussed in Section 2.1 from comparable corpora, 2) Prune the candidate lists by ranking items, this is done using a Machine Learning (ML) algorithm trained over parallel corpora for detecting the outliers, discussed in Section 2.2;

The initial frequency lists for alignment are based Wikipedia dumps for the following languages: **Romance** (French, Italian, Spanish, Portuguese) and **Slavonic** (Bulgarian, Russian, Ukrainian), where the target languages are Spanish and Russian[1].

2.1 Cognate detection

We extract possible lists of cognates from comparable corpora by using a family of similarity measures:

L direct matching between the languages using Levenshtein distance (Levenshtein, 1966); $L(w_s, w_t) = 1 - ed(w_s, w_t)$

L-R Levenshtein distance with weights computed separately for the roots and for the endings; $LR(r_s, r_t, e_s, e_t) = \frac{\alpha \times ed(r_s, r_t) + \beta \times ed(e_s, e_t)}{\alpha + \beta}$

L-C Levenshtein distance over word with similar number of starting characters (i.e. prefix);

$$LC(c_s, c_t) = \begin{cases} 1 - ed(c_s, c_t), & \text{same prefix} \\ 0, & \text{otherwise} \end{cases}$$

where $ed(.,.)$ is the normalised Levenshtein distance in characters between the source word w_s and the target word w_t. The r_s and r_t are the stems produced by the Snowball stemmer[2] . Since the Snowball stemmer does not support Ukrainian and Bulgarian, we used the Russian model for making the stem/ending split. e_s, e_t are the characters at the end of a word form given a stem and c_s, c_t are the first n characters of a word. In this work, we set the weights $\alpha = 0.6$ and $\beta = 0.4$ giving more importance to the roots. We set a higher weight to roots on the **L-R**, which is language dependent, and compare to the **L-C** metric, which is language independent. We transform the Levenshtein distances into similarity metrics by subtracting the normalised distance score from one.

The produced lists contain for each source word the possible n-best target words accordingly to the maximum scores with one of the previous measures. The n-best list allows possible cognate translations to a given source word that share a part of the surface form. Different from (Mann and Yarowsky, 2001), we produce n-best cognate lists scored by edit distance instead of 1-best. An important problem when comparing comparable corpora is the way of representing the search space, where an exhaustive method compares all the combinations of source and target words (Mann and Yarowsky, 2001). We constraint the search space by comparing each source word against the target words that belong to a frequency window around the frequency of the source word. This constraint only applies for the **L** and **L-R** metrics. We use Wikipedia dumps for the source and target side processed in the form frequency lists. We order the target side list into bins of similar frequency and for the source side we filter words that appear only once. We use the window approach given that the frequency between the corpora under study can not be directly comparable. During testing we use a wide window of ± 200 bins to minimise the loss of good candidate translations. The second search space constraint heuristic is the **L-C** metric. This metric only compares source words with the target words upto a given n prefix. For c_s, c_t in **L-C** , we use the first four characters to compare groups of words as suggested in (Kondrak et al., 2003).

2.2 Cognate Ranking

Given that the n-best lists contain noise, we aim to prune them by an ML ranking model. However, there is a lack of resources to train a classification model for cognates (i.e. cognate vs. false friend), as mentioned in (Fišer and Ljubešić, 2013). Available data that can be used to judge the cognate lists are the alignment pairs extracted from parallel data. We decide to use a ranking model to avoid data imbalance present in classification and to use the probability scores of the alignment pairs as

[1]For the Slavonic family we only use languages based on the Cyrillic alphabet to avoid the character set problems.

[2]`http://snowball.tartarus.org/`

ranks, as opposed to the classification model used by (Irvine and Callison-Burch, 2013). Moreover, we also use a popular domain adaptation technique (Daumé et al., 2010) given that we have access to different domains of parallel training data that might be compatible with our comparable corpora.

The training data are the alignments between pairs of words where we rank them accordingly to their correspondent alignment probability from the output of GIZA++ (Och and Ney, 2003). We then use a heuristic to prune training data in order to simulate cognate words. Pairs of words scored below the Levenshtein similarity threshold of 0.5 are not considered as cognates given that they are likely to have a different surface form.

We represent the training and test data with features extracted from different edit distance scores and distributional measures. The edit distances features are as follows: 1) Similarity measure **L** and 2) Number of times of each edit operation. Thus, the model assigns a different importance to each operation. The distributional feature is based on the cosine between the distributional vectors of a window of n words around the word currently under comparison. We train distributional similarity models with word2vec (Mikolov et al., 2013a) for the source and target side separately. We extract the continuous vector for each word in the window, concatenate it and then compute the cosine between the concatenated vectors of the source and the target. We suspect that the vectors will have similar behaviour between the source and the target given that they are trained under parallel Wikipedia articles. We develop two ML models: 1) Edit distance scores and 2) Edit distance scores and distributional similarity score.

We use SVMlight (Joachims, 1998) for the ranking model with the augmented features for domain adaptation. The domains are as follows: Wikipedia aligned titles, open source subtitles and proprietary subtitles, discussed in Section 3.1.

3 Results and Discussion

In this section we describe the data used to produce the n-best lists and train the cognate ranking models. We evaluate the ranking models with heldout data from each training domain. We also provide manual evaluation over the ranked n-best lists for error analysis.

3.1 Data

The n-best lists to detect cognates were extracted from the respective Wikipedias by using the method described in Section 2.1. The training data for the ranking model consists of different types of parallel corpora. The parallel corpora are as follows: 1) **Wiki-titles** we use the inter language links to create a parallel corpus from the tittles of the Wikipedia articles, with about 500K aligned links (i.e. 'sentences') per language pair (about 200k for bg-ru), giving us about 200K training instances per language pair [3], 2) **Opensubs** is an open source corpus of subtitles built by the fan community, with 1M sentences, 6M tokens, 100K words, giving about 90K training instances (Tiedemann, 2012) and 3) **Zoo** is a proprietary corpus of subtitles produced by professional translators, with 100K sentences, 700K tokens, 40K words and giving about 20K training instances per language pair.

Our objective is to create MT dictionaries from the produced n-best lists and we use parallel data as a source of training to prune them. We are interested in the corpora of subtitles because the chosen domain of our SMT experiments is subtitling, while the proposed ranking method can be used in other application domains as well.

We consider Zoo and Opensubs as two different domains given that they were built by different types of translators and they differ in size and quality. The heldout data consists of 2K instances for each corpus.

We use Wikipedia documents and Opensusbs subtitles to train word2vec for the distributional similarity feature. We use the continuous bag-of-words algorithm for word2vec and set the parameters for training to 200 dimensions and a window of 8 words. The Wikipedia documents with an average number of 70K documents for each language, and Opensubs subtitles with 1M sentences for each language. In practice we only use the Wikipedia data given that for Opensubs the model is able to find relatively few vectors, for example a vector is found only for 20% of the words in the pt-es pair.

3.2 Evaluation of the Ranking Model

We define two ranking models as: model *E* for edit distance features and model *EC* for both edit

[3]The aligned links have been extracted with: https://github.com/clab/wikipedia-parallel-titles

	Zoo error%		Opensubs error%		Wiki-titles error%	
Lang pairs	Model E	Model EC	Model E	Model EC	Model E	Model EC
Romance						
pt-es	53.31	53.72	54.81	48.31	12.22	9.87
it-es	56.00	42.86	63.95	63.03	8.44	11.23
fr-es	59.05	53.00	43.00	41.19	10.75	10.09
Slavonic						
uk-ru	47.90	40.84	37.06	30.19	10.71	10.72
bg-ru	54.17	43.98	49.12	57.89	18.72	17.13

Table 1: Zero/one-error percentage results on heldout test parallel data for each training domain.

distance and distributional similarity features. We evaluate these models with heldout data from each domain used for training. Each test dataset is evaluated with Zero/one-error percentage, that is the fraction of perfectly correct rankings. We evaluate the models for the Romance and Slavonic families where the target languages are Spanish and Russian respectively.

Table 1 shows the results of the ranking procedure. For the Romance family language pairs the model *EC* with context features consistently reduces the error compared to the solely use of edit distance metrics. The only exception is the it-es *EC* model with poor results for the domain of Wiki-titles. The models for the Slavonic family behave similarly to the Romance family, where the use of context features reduces the ranking error. The exception is the bg-ru model on the Opensubs domain.

A possible reason for the poor results on the it-es and bg-ru models is that the model often assigns a high similarity score to unrelated words. For example, in it-es, *mortes* 'deads' is treated as close to *categoria* 'category'. A possible solution is to map the vectors form the source side into the space of the target side via a learned transformation matrix (Mikolov et al., 2013b).

3.3 Preliminary Results on Comparable Corpora

After we extracted the n-best lists for the Romance family comparable corpora, we applied one of the ranking models on these lists and we manually evaluated over a sample of 50 words[4]. We set n to 10 for the n-best lists. We use a frequency window of 200 for the n-best list search heuristic and the domain of the comparable corpora to Wiki-titles for the domain adaptation technique. The purpose of manual evaluation is to decide whether the ML setup is sensible on the objective task. Each list is evaluated by accuracy at 1 and accuracy at 10. We also show success and failure examples of the ranking and the n-best lists. Table 2 shows the preliminary results of the ML model *E* on a sample of Wikipedia dumps. The **L** and **L-R** lists consistently show poor results. A possible reason is the amount of errors given the first step to extract the n-best lists. For example, in pt-es, for the word *vivem* 'live' the 10-best list only contain one word with a similar meaning *viva* 'living' but it can be also translated as 'cheers'.

In the pt-es list for the word *representação* 'description' the correct translation *representación* is not among the 10-best in the **L** list. However, it is present in the 10-best for the **L-C** list and the ML model *EC* ranks it in the first place. The edit distance model *E* still makes mistakes like with the list **L-C**, the word *vivem* 'live' translates into *viven* 'living' and the correct translation is *vivir*. However, given a certain context/sense the previous translation can be correct. The ranking scores given by the SVM varies from each list version. For the **L-C** lists the scores are more uniform in increasing order and with a small variance. The **L** and **L-R** lists show the opposite behaviour.

We add the produced Wikipedia n-best lists with the **L** metric into a SMT training dataset for the pt-es pair. We use the Moses SMT toolkit (Koehn et al., 2007) to test the augmented datasets. We compare the augmented model with a baseline both trained by using the Zoo corpus of subtitles. We use a 1-best list consisting of 100K pairs. Te dataset used for pt-es baseline is: 80K training sentences, 1K sentences for tuning and 2K sen-

[4]The sample consists of words with a frequency between 2K and 5.

	List L		List L-R		List L-C	
Lang Pairs	acc@1	acc@10	acc@1	acc@10	acc@1	acc@10
pt-es	20	60	22	59	32	70
it-es	16	53	18	45	44	66
fr-es	10	48	12	51	29	59

Table 2: Accuracy at 1 and at 10 results of the ML model E over a sample of 50 words on Wikipedia dumps comparable corpora for the Romance family.

tences for testing. We use fast-align[5], KenLM[6] with a 5-gram language model and Moses with the standard feature set . The BLEU score for the baseline is 20.68 and 20.86 for the augmented version, where the +0.18 increase is not statistically significant. However, the augmented dataset improves the coverage of the model. The out of vocabulary (OOV) words decrease from: 1476 tokens (9.4%), 623 types (21.1%) to 896 tokens (5.7%) and 337 types (11.4%). For uk-ru the baseline training data is: 140K training sentences, 1K sentences for tuning and 2K sentences for testing. The uk-ru 1-best list consists of 100K. The BLEU results for the baseline is 28.72 and 29.56 for the augmented dataset with a difference in +0.93 which is not statistically significant[7]. The results for OOV are: 1202 tokens (8.1%), 756 types (21.6%) to 894 tokens (6.0%) and 545 types (15.6%).

A possible reason for low improvement in terms of the BLEU scores is because MT evaluation metrics, such as BLEU, compare the MT output with a human reference. The human reference translations in our corpus have been done from English (e.g., En→Es), while the test translations come from a related language (En→Pt→Es), often resulting in different paraphrases of the same English source. While our OOV rate improved, the evaluation scores did not reflected this, because our MT output was still far from the reference even in cases it was otherwise acceptable.

4 Conclusions and future Work

We have presented work in progress for developing MT dictionaries extracted from comparable resources for related languages. The extraction heuristic show positive results on the n-best lists that group words with the same starting characters, because the used comparable corpora consist of related languages that share a similar orthography. However, the lists based on the frequency window heuristic show poor results to include the correct translations during the extraction step. Our ML models based on similarity metrics over parallel corpora show rankings similar to heldout data. However, we created our training data using simple heuristics that simulate cognate words (i.e. pairs of words with a small surface difference). The ML models are able to rank similar words on the top of the list and they give a reliable score to discriminate wrong translations. Preliminary results on the addition of the n-best lists into an SMT system show modest improvements compare to the baseline. However, the OOV rate shows improvements around 10% reduction on word types, because of the wide variety of lexical choices introduced by the MT dictionaries.

Future work involves the addition of unsupervised morphology features for the n-best list extraction, i.e. first step, given that the use of starting characters shows to be an effective heuristic to prune the search space and language independent. Finally, we will measure the contribution for all the produced cognate lists, where we can try different strategies to add the dictionaries into an SMT system (Irvine and Callison-Burch, 2014).

Acknowledgments

The research was funded by Innovate UK and ZOO Digital Group plc.

References

Hal Daumé, III, Abhishek Kumar, and Avishek Saha. 2010. Frustratingly easy semi-supervised domain adaptation. In *Proceedings of the 2010 Workshop on Domain Adaptation for Natural Language Processing*, DANLP 2010, pages 53–59, Stroudsburg, PA, USA.

Darja Fišer and Nikola Ljubešić. 2013. Best friends or just faking it? Corpus-based extraction of Slovene-

[5]https://github.com/clab/fast_align

[6]https://kheafield.com/code/kenlm/

[7]The p-value for the uk-ru pair is 0.06 we do not consider this result as statistically significant.

Croatian translation equivalents and false friends. *Slovenščina 2.0*, 1.

Oana Frunza and Diana Inkpen. 2009. Identification and disambiguation of cognates, false friends, and partial cognates using machine learning techniques. *International Journal of Linguistics*, 1(1).

Ann Irvine and Chris Callison-Burch. 2013. Supervised bilingual lexicon induction with multiple monolingual signals. In *Proceedings of the 2013 Conference of the North American Chapter of the Association for Computational Linguistics (NAACL 2013)*, Atlanta, Georgia, June.

Ann Irvine and Chris Callison-Burch. 2014. Using comparable corpora to adapt mt models to new domains. In *Proceedings of the Ninth Workshop on Statistical Machine Translation*, pages 437–444, June.

Sittichai Jiampojamarn, Colin Cherry, and Grzegorz Kondrak. 2010. Integrating joint n-gram features into a discriminative training framework. In *Proceedings of NAACL-2010*, Los Angeles, CA, June.

T. Joachims. 1998. Making large-scale svm learning practical. LS8-Report 24, Universität Dortmund, LS VIII-Report.

Philipp Koehn, Hieu Hoang, Alexandra Birch, Chris Callison-Burch, Marcello Federico, Nicola Bertoldi, Brooke Cowan, Wade Shen, Christine Moran, Richard Zens, Chris Dyer, Ondřej Bojar, Alexandra Constantin, and Evan Herbst. 2007. Moses: Open source toolkit for statistical machine translation. In *Proceedings of the 45th Annual Meeting of the ACL on Interactive Poster and Demonstration Sessions*, ACL '07, pages 177–180, Stroudsburg, PA, USA.

Grzegorz Kondrak, Daniel Marcu, and Kevin Knight. 2003. Cognates can improve statistical translation models. In *Proceedings of the 2003 Conference of the North American Chapter of the Association for Computational Linguistics on Human Language Technology: Companion Volume of the Proceedings of HLT-NAACL 2003–short Papers - Volume 2*, pages 46–48, Stroudsburg, PA, USA.

Vladimir Iosifovich Levenshtein. 1966. Binary codes capable of correcting deletions, insertions, and reversals. *Soviet Physics Doklady*, 10:707–710.

Gideon S. Mann and David Yarowsky. 2001. Multipath translation lexicon induction via bridge languages. In *Proceedings of NAACL*, page 151–158, Pittsburgh, PA, June.

Tomas Mikolov, Kai Chen, Greg Corrado, and Jeffrey Dean. 2013a. Efficient estimation of word representations in vector space. In *Proc. Workshop at ICLR'13*.

Tomas Mikolov, Quoc V. Le, and Ilya Sutskever. 2013b. Exploiting similarities among languages for machine translation. *CoRR*, abs/1309.4168.

Franz Josef Och and Hermann Ney. 2003. A systematic comparison of various statistical alignment models. *Computational Linguistics*, 29(1):19–51.

Serge Sharoff, Reinhard Rapp, and Pierre Zweigenbaum. 2013. Overviewing important aspects of the last twenty years of research in comparable corpora. In Serge Sharoff, Reinhard Rapp, Pierre Zweigenbaum, and Pascale Fung, editors, *BUCC: Building and Using Comparable Corpora*, pages 1–17. Springer.

Jörg Tiedemann. 1999. Automatic construction of weighted similarity measures. In *Proc. Empirical methods in Natural Language Processing and Very Large Corpora*, pages 213–219.

Jorg Tiedemann. 2012. Parallel data, tools and interfaces in opus. In *Proceedings of the Eight International Conference on Language Resources and Evaluation (LREC'12)*, Istanbul, Turkey, may.

BUCC Shared Task: Cross-Language Document Similarity

Serge Sharoff
University of Leeds
Leeds, UK
s.sharoff@leeds.ac.uk

Pierre Zweigenbaum
LIMSI, CNRS
Orsay, France
pz@limsi.fr

Reinhard Rapp
University of Mainz
Mainz, Germany
reinhardrapp@gmx.de

Abstract

We summarise the organisation and results of the first shared task aimed at detecting the most similar texts in a large multilingual collection. The dataset of the shared was based on Wikipedia dumps with interlanguage links with further filtering to ensure comparability of the paired articles. The eleven system runs we received have been evaluated using the TREC evaluation metrics.

1 Task description

Parallel corpora of original texts with their translations provide the basis for multilingual NLP applications since the beginning of the 1990s. Relative scarcity of such resources led to greater attention to comparable (=less parallel) resources to mine information about possible translations. Many studies have been produced within the paradigm of comparable corpora, including publications in the BUCC workshop series since 2008.[1]

However, the community so far has not conducted an evaluation which compared different approaches for identifying more or less parallel documents in a large amount of multilingual data. Also, it is not clear how language-specific such approaches are. In this shared task we propose the first evaluation exercise, which is aimed at detecting the most similar texts in a large multilingual collection.

2 Data set

2.1 Description

The dataset is derived from static Wikipedia dumps of the main articles. A feature of Wikipedia is that it provides so-called inter-language links between many corresponding articles of different languages, i.e. between articles describing the same or corresponding headwords. These interlanguage links are provided by the authors of the articles, i.e. they are based on expert judgement. For the shared task we selected bilingual pairs of articles which fulfilled the following requirements:

1. The inter-language links between the articles had to be bidirectional, i.e. not only an article in Language_1 needs to be linked to the corresponding article in Language_2, but also vice versa. This ensured a page in one language is not linked only to a portion of a page in another one.
2. The size of the textual content of the two articles within a pair (i.e. their length measured as the number of characters) had to be similar (see Section 2.2 below).

Note that this selection procedure for the article pairs implies that an article pair selected for one language pair may or may not be selected for another language pair. All articles which satisfied the selection conditions have been considered for the evaluation run.

The data for each language pair has been split randomly into two sets:

Training set articles with information about the correct links for the respective language pairs provided to the participants;

Test set articles without the links.

The task is for each article in the test set to submit up to five ranked suggestions to its linked article, assuming that the gold standard contains its counterpart in another language. The submissions had to be in the tab-separated format as used in the submissions to the shared tasks of the Text Retrieval Conference (TREC[2]) with six fields:

[1]See http://comparable.limsi.fr/

[2]See http://trec.nist.gov/.

Shared Task Paper Proceedings of the Eighth Workshop on Building and Using Comparable Corpora, pages 74–77,
Beijing, China, July 30, 2015.

	Min.	1st Qu	Median	Mean	3rd Qu	Max.	Selected pairs
De	0.010	0.420	0.790	1.244	1.370	206.000	294990
Fr	0.000	0.370	0.740	1.194	1.260	255.800	229591
Ru	0.010	0.300	0.620	0.987	1.070	108.600	159810
Tr	0.000	0.140	0.350	0.616	0.760	46.730	32614
Zh	0.010	0.280	0.610	1.010	1.090	111.500	42944

Table 1: Ratios of lengths of aligned articles to English

```
id1 X id2 Y score run.name
```

The X and Y fields are not used, but they are reserved by the TREC evaluation script (and it does not use them either). `id1` and `id2` are the respective article identifiers in a source language and in English. The *score* should reflect the similarity between `id1` and `id2`, the higher the closer. The participants were invited to submit up to five runs of their system with different parameters, as identified by a keyword in the last field.

The evaluation script and more information about the format have been made available in advance. [3]

The languages in the shared task were Chinese, French, German, Russian and Turkish. Pages in these languages needed to be linked to a page in English.

The choice of languages reflects variation in the available clues for linking the pages. The languages vary in:

- their writing systems (Latin, Cyrillic, logographic);
- tokenisation (clitics in French, compounds in German, no orthographic word boundaries in Chinese);
- their morphology (covering isolating, inflecting and agglutinative languages);

Even though the writing system issue is superficial, it shifts the clues for linking the articles. Thus, it requires more intelligent mapping between the languages. In the same writing system, many clues remain the same or nearly identical (*Paris, Frankfurt*), while in another set they have to adapt to the target language requirements: Париж ('Paris', transliterated as *Parizh* in Russian) or 巴黎 ('Paris', pinyin *Bali* in Chinese).

Morphology accounts for variation of forms for connection with the dictionaries. It is considerably larger in morphologically rich languages, such as Russian or Turkish. Therefore, mapping of word forms is likely to be more sparse.

[3] See `http://trec.nist.gov/trec_eval/`

2.2 Preparation

We started with the downloadable Wikipedia dumps,[4] which were cleaned to their text only contents by removing standard formatting codes, figures (with their captions), templates, tables and external links. Given that the first sentence in Wikipedia articles provide a concise summary of the article contents, the first sentence (defined as a sequence of characters to the first full stop) has been also removed to make the task more similar to detection of webpages in context unrelated to Wikipedia. Shaded areas in Figure 1 demonstrate the extent of cleaning.

We selected a subset of articles aligned to English. Table 1 lists the distribution of the length ratios of the respective articles to their English counterparts and the number of articles remaining after pruning their length. A small number of articles are much shorter than their English counterparts. Less frequently this happens in the opposite direction, and the length ratio is more than one (the median is always less than one). Usually articles which differ in their length are not good candidates for comparable corpora. We took only those within the inter-quartile range. This left us with 50% of article pairs in the original list, which are all reasonably comparable in their contents. Examples for each language bordering on the 1st quartile in ratio to English all show reasonable amount of text to be considered as comparable entries:

de *Aaron Ramsey*
fr *Adena culture*
ru *Quantum mechanics*
tr *Cyrano de Bergerac (play)*
zh *Blood transfusion*

[4] Downloaded in November 2011.

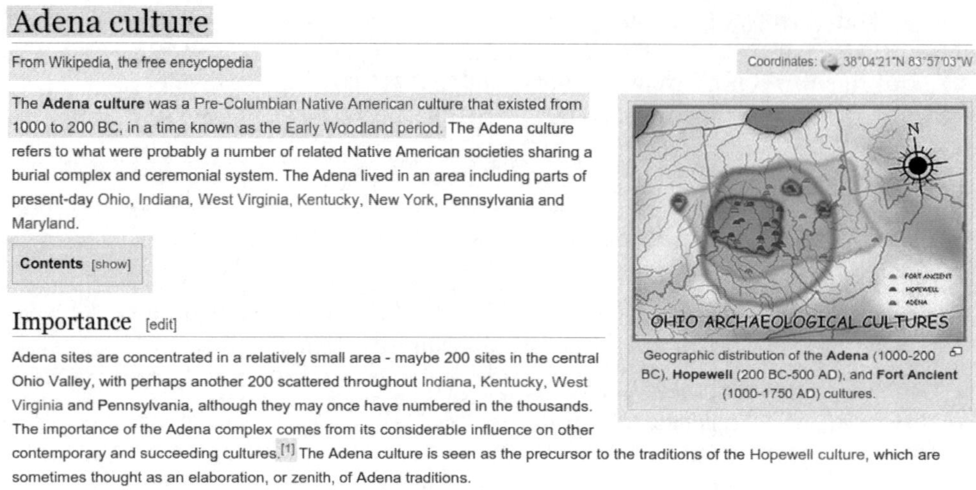

Adena culture

From Wikipedia, the free encyclopedia

Coordinates: 38°04′21″N 83°57′03″W

The **Adena culture** was a Pre-Columbian Native American culture that existed from 1000 to 200 BC, in a time known as the Early Woodland period. The Adena culture refers to what were probably a number of related Native American societies sharing a burial complex and ceremonial system. The Adena lived in an area including parts of present-day Ohio, Indiana, West Virginia, Kentucky, New York, Pennsylvania and Maryland.

Contents [show]

Geographic distribution of the **Adena** (1000-200 BC), **Hopewell** (200 BC-500 AD), and **Fort Ancient** (1000-1750 AD) cultures.

Importance [edit]

Adena sites are concentrated in a relatively small area - maybe 200 sites in the central Ohio Valley, with perhaps another 200 scattered throughout Indiana, Kentucky, West Virginia and Pennsylvania, although they may once have numbered in the thousands. The importance of the Adena complex comes from its considerable influence on other contemporary and succeeding cultures.[1] The Adena culture is seen as the precursor to the traditions of the Hopewell culture, which are sometimes thought as an elaboration, or zenith, of Adena traditions.

Figure 1: Example of cleanup (shaded areas indicate removed text).

For example, the *Adena culture* article has been selected only for the French-English pair, since the articles in other languages are much shorter than the English one to be considered as reasonably comparable.

3 Evaluation

Evaluation has been done using standard TREC evaluation measures, modeling the task as the retrieval of a ranked list of links from a source page.

Extrinsic evaluation setups, for example, via terminology extraction, would possibly provide more interesting measures, but this would require a baseline system which works with all the languages in question.

3.1 Metrics

For each source page there exists exactly one correct linked page in the gold standard. Systems were required to return a ranked list of hypotheses in which the correct target page should be ranked as high as possible.

Several evaluation measures are relevant to this situation in the `trec_eval` program used in TREC evaluations. The *Success* measures correspond to commonly used measures when evaluating term translations in comparable corpora. We use them here to evaluate the proposed interlanguage links between the articles. Success@1 determines the proportion of source articles for which the correct target article has been ranked in the top position; Success@5 determines the proportion of source articles for which the correct target article has been ranked among the top 5 positions. *Mean Reciprocal Rank* (MRR) is also a relevant measure: If the correct target article is ranked at position N, a score of $1/N$ is given to this source article. Then these scores are averaged over the set of source articles. These measures are respectively obtained by parameters `success.1`, `success.5`, and `recip_rank` in `trec_eval`.

4 Results

Overall, we have received eleven runs: one entry for Chinese (Table 2), three entries for French (Table 2), and seven for German (Table 3).

4.1 Methods used

The method used by the system CCNUNLP is described in (Li and Gaussier, 2013). In essence, it uses a bilingual dictionary for converting the word feature vectors between the languages and estimating their overlap. The other systems are discussed in details in the current proceedings (Morin et al., 2015; Zafarian et al., 2015). The LINA system (Morin et al., 2015) is based on matching hapax legomena, i.e., words occurring only once. In addition to using hapax legomena, the quality of linking in one language pair, e.g., French-English, is also assessed by using information available in pages in another language pair, e.g., German-English. The AUT system (Zafarian et al., 2015) uses the most complicated setup by combining several steps. First, documents in different languages are mapped into the same space using a

	French			Chinese
runid	ccnunlp	lina.p	lina.cl	ccnunlp
num_q	114423	114423	78529	21467
num_ret	572115	572111	143542	107335
num_rel	114423	114423	78529	21467
num_rel_ret	87367	42777	47561	18474
MRR	0.669	0.329	0.590	0.769
success@1	0.607	0.300	0.577	0.710
success@5	0.764	0.374	0.606	0.861

Table 2: Evaluation results for French and Chinese. `lina.p` corresponds to Pigeonhole, `lina.cl` to Cross-lingual in the authors' paper.

	German						
runid	lina.p	lina.cl	aut1	aut2	aut3	aut4	aut5
num_q	147220	92020	147515	147515	147515	147515	147515
num_ret	736100	166051	147516	147516	147516	147516	147516
num_rel	147220	92020	147515	147515	147515	147515	147515
num_rel_ret	52223	58828	6870	2703	2029	1371	890
MRR	0.290	0.622	0.047	0.018	0.014	0.009	0.006
success@1	0.249	0.607	0.047	0.018	0.014	0.009	0.006
success@5	0.355	0.639	0.047	0.018	0.014	0.009	0.006

Table 3: Evaluation results for German

feature transformation matrix. This helps in selecting a relatively small subset of pages to detect possible links. Second, document similarity is assessed using three pipelines, namely, a polylingual topic model, a named entities detection tool and a word feature mapping procedure using MT.

4.2 Comparison of results

Since AUT submitted exactly one target article for each source article, its MRR, success@1 and success@5 measures are identical.

For each run, success@1 is the strictest measure, hence provides the lowest score, because it can only obtain points if the top ranked article is the correct one. Mean reciprocal rank (MRR) yields the same score when the top ranked article is correct, but also scores decreasing fractions of one when the correct article is found anywhere in the ranking: this results in a higher average score than success@1. Finally, success@5 also takes into account articles beyond the first, but only until the fifth; if the correct article is present in this range, the full score of one is assigned to the article; otherwise no point is obtained. Therefore a system which generally ranks correct articles beyond the fifth position will have a lower success@5 than its MRR; but a system which ranks correct articles before the sixth position often enough will have a higher success@5 than MRR. This is the case of all systems except aut, which only returned one target article per source article.

The tables show that the rankings obtained by the three measures, MRR, success@1 and success@5 are the same in all cases, i.e., rank correlation of the results is always 1. This suggests that system results ranked the correct article in the top 5 often enough.

4.3 Comparison of methods

The best results were obtained on Chinese with a succes@1 of 0.710 and a success@5 of 0.861. This is a very good performance, but also reveals that the problem is not solved.

Although the number of different runs is not sufficient to draw general conclusions, we can compare the same methods across different language pairs and different methods on the same language pairs.

CCNUNLP obtained better results on Chinese than on French, probably because of the quality of the underlying dictionaries. LINA.CL worked better on German than for French, while the reverse was true for LINA.P. After the evaluation run, it transpired that the submissions of AUT had a data processing bug.

Overall, the CCNUNLP method obtained the best results on Chinese and French, followed by the LINA.CL method (second best on French, and best on German).

4.4 Discussion

The results are encouraging. Success@1 rates reach 0.71 for Chinese and 0.61 for French and German. However, this level of accuracy is still far from reliable identification of comparable pages. Given a small number of participating systems and an uneven coverage of the language pairs involved it is difficult to make predictions about which methods are more or less successful. A dictionary-based method (CCNUNLP) is slightly ahead of a method based on hapax legomena (LINA.*). A multi-stage method like the one used by AUT is promising, but its complexity makes it prone to errors.

Another question concerns the evaluation scenario. The shared task has been evaluated by using gold standard data in intrinsic evaluation. Given that the purpose of collecting comparable corpora is to provide more data for terminology extraction or Machine Translation, we need to evaluate text collections by referring to their successful use in such tasks. The limitation in using extrinsic evaluation is the lack of gold-standard methods and resources.

In the next shared task we plan to address this issue by specifically targeting either terminology extraction or MT development methods by using comparable corpora. This shared task will use the resources we developed for the current one.

4.5 Conclusions

In addition to obtaining an estimate of the quality of various methods for measuring comparability, the major outcomes of the evaluation exercise concerns the available standardised dataset which is split into the training and testing parts. We encourage our readers to develop better systems and to test them on our data. The dataset is available from:

`http://corpus.leeds.ac.uk/serge/BUCC/`

We intend to keep the data on the web for many years as a benchmark for measuring comparability on the text level.

References

Li, B. and Gaussier, E. (2013). Exploiting comparable corpora for lexicon extraction: Measuring and improving corpus quality. In Sharoff, S., Rapp, R., Zweigenbaum, P., and Fung, P., editors, *Building and Using Comparable Corpora*, pages 131–149. Springer-Verlag.

Morin, E., Hazem, A., Boudin, F., and Loginova-Clouet, E. (2015). Lina: Identifying comparable documents from wikipedia. In *Proc. Workshop on Building and Using Comparable Corpora at ACL 2015*.

Zafarian, A., Agha Sadeghi, A. P., Azadi, F., Ghiasifard, S., Ali Panahloo, Z., bakhshaei, S., and Mohammadzadeh Ziabary, S. M. (2015). Aut document alignment framework for bucc workshop shared task. In *Proc. Workshop on Building and Using Comparable Corpora at ACL 2015*.

AUT Document Alignment Framework for BUCC Workshop Shared Task

Atefeh Zafarian, Amirpouya Aghasadeghi, Fatemeh Azadi,
Sonia Ghiasifard, Zeinab Alipanahloo, Somayeh Bakhshaei,
Seyed Mohammad Mohammadzadeh Ziabary
Human Language Technology Lab
Computer Engineering Department
Amirkabir University of Technology, Tehran, Iran
{atefeh.zafarian, aghasadeghi, ft.azadi, s.ghiasi,
apanahloo, bakhshaei, mehran.m}@aut.ac.ir

Abstract

This paper presents a framework for aligning comparable documents collection. Our feature based model is able to consider different characteristics of documents for evaluating their similarities. The model uses the content of documents while no link, special tag or Metadata are available. And also we apply a filtering mechanism which made our model to be properly applicable for a large collection of data. According to the results, our model is able to recognize related documents in the target language with recall of 45.67% for the 1-best and 62% for the 5-best.

1 Introduction

Comparable corpora (CC) are collections of similar documents with different levels of comparability (Fung and Cheung, 2004). There are useful resources for most of the Natural Language Processing (NLP) or Information Retrieval (IR) tasks such as cross-lingual text mining (Tang et al., 2011), bilingual lexicon extraction (Li and Gaussier, 2010), cross-lingual information retrieval (Knoth et al., 2011) and machine translation (Smith et al., 2010; Delpech, 2011) etc.

The sub-fields of NLP are related to solving human language tasks that are mostly hard problems such as Language Understanding (Winograd, 1972), Machine Translation etc. The modern algorithms of NLP sub-fields are based on machine learning and statistical approaches. Most of the developed systems of these fields require large amounts of parallel corpora, as a result the limitation in success of such tasks is the lack of parallel corpora. In recent researches, it is proven that Comparable Corpora can be a valuable alternative to rare parallel corpora.

Information Retrieval (IR) is "the act of finding materials, usually documents of an unstructured form that satisfies an information need within large collections stored in computers" (Manning et al., 2008). IR is not limited to monolingual documents if the task is related to mapping bilingual or multilingual documents; a new area of IR will be introduced: Cross/Multilingual IR. The idea of Cross-Lingual IR (CLIR) is to retrieve documents in a language different from the language of input text (Oard, 1998). The input text may be either a query or a document which categorizes the field to document based or query based approaches. CLIR is a way of expanding input queries to other languages. This is a useful approach in search engines that enables users to formulate queries in their preferred languages and retrieve relevant documents in whatever language they are written. For this purpose instead of parallel corpora for translating input queries, using comparable corpora might be helpful. However, document based CLIR can be used for producing comparable corpora. The related works will be reviewed in section 2.

Our Model is a framework consists of different modules. Each module considers disparate features for matching each source document with the target documents, so we called this a feature-based model. The pipeline of the modules in our model is shown in Figure 1.

We assume two similar documents contain same sets of names which occur in the same order. Name Module of our model is responsible for checking this structure. In addition, translation of similar texts in the source and target languages must be similar, so we use SMT system as another module in the model. We also assume similar documents converted to vector representations using neural networks will have shorter Euclidean distance between each other. This characteristic of similar documents is considered

Shared Task Paper Proceedings of the Eighth Workshop on Building and Using Comparable Corpora, pages 79–87,
Beijing, China, July 30, 2015. ©2015 Association for Computational Linguistics

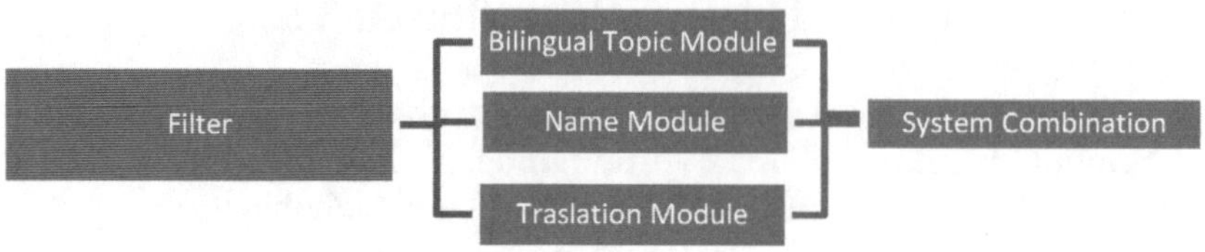

Figure 1. The structure of the pipeline model.

in Document-to-Vector module. To recognize similar conceptual structures in documents we use bilingual topic models.

The problem is aligning source documents to target documents, but because of the amount of data, in addition to similarity concerns, our model is faced to the very large corpora problem. It is not possible to evaluate each pair of documents in this big space, so we used some of our modules as a filter for decreasing the target space. From the framework's modules, we choose ones with higher Recall to be sure that our filter is able to recognize and remove wrong samples. Another factor for selecting the filtering modules is the execution speed. Low speed modules are not proper in the model's pipeline.

2 Related Works

Common methods for comparing documents are by extracting features from texts; namely compare documents through the most frequent words (Kilgarriff, 2001).

In multilingual context, some approaches translate features and compare documents using differences in the frequencies of the translations of the keywords, namely using cosine similarity measure between the feature vectors (Su and Babych, 2012).

A successful approach is the Cross Language Character N-Gram (CL-CNG) model (Mcnamee and Mayfield, 2004) that uses character n-grams and is based on the syntax of documents, found remarkable performance for languages with syntactic similarities.

A primary approach for aligning comparable document corpora is based on statistical machine translation technology such as CL-ASA (Barrón-Cedeno et al., 2008), that uses a combination of a translation model and a length model for measuring similarity between source and target documents. The translation model shows that how likely the source document is a translation of the target document and length model measures the similarity of those two documents with the length attribute. It is expected for a pair of translated documents to have closely related lengths.

A common language independent approach for representing documents is based on vector representation. Representing documents in a collection as bag off words is called Vector Space Model. Each component of the vector shows the importance of that term in the document. In large document collections, document vectors have high dimensions. For this reason, some approaches using linear projection, a map from the high dimension to a low-dimensional vector space. Early approaches for linear projection are LSA (Deerwester et al., 1990) and LDA (Blei et al., 2003).

Cross-language latent semantic indexing (CL-LSI) (Dumais et al., 1997) is based on LSA used for multiple languages by reducing the dimensionality of a matrix which rows are obtained by concatenating comparable documents from different languages. Another projection model, Latent Dirichlet Allocation (LDA) is based on the extraction of generative models from documents. Polylingual Topic Models (Mimno et al., 2009) are multilingual versions of LDA.

Cross Language Explicit Semantic Analysis (CL-ESA) is the other model in vector context approach (Potthast et al., 2008) that uses comparable Wikipedia corpora. Each document is represented by a concept vector, where each dimension is the similarity of the document to one of the Wikipedia documents in the corpus.

New approaches for comparable document retrieval task and for measuring documents similarities are knowledge-based; despite previous works that were supervised. Knowledge-based Document Similarity (KBSim) (Franco-Salvador et al., 2008) is one of the most recent of them. It turns source and target documents to knowledge graphs using a Multilingual Semantic Network (MSN) such as Babelnet (Navigli and Ponzetto, 2012) then compares two graphs using KBSim.

3 Model description

The framework of our model is constructed on 4 modules: Doc2Vec, Name, Topic Model and SMT. These modules evaluate the similarity of each pair of documents considering different characteristics of a document pair.

According to the framework of our model (Figure 1), the first step contains filters for reducing the size of the target space. Two filters are used serially based on Doc2Vec and Name modules for this purpose. In the following subsections, we explain each of the modules used in our framework in more details.

3.1 Document-to-Vector Module (Doc2Vec)

Recent works in learning vector representation of words using neural networks (Mikolov et al., 2013), show that these models can capture great details about semantics and syntactic relationships and patterns between similar words, which many of those patterns can be obtained from simple linear transitions. For example, it has been shown that the result of a vector calculation vec("Madrid") - vec("Spain") + vec("France") is closer to vec("Paris") than to any other word vector (Mikolov et al., 2013).

Another great properties of these models is that if they trained on comparable corpora in different languages, by using simple transformation matrix, vectors from source language can be projected to the target space and be used to build a larger dictionary (Mikolov et al., 2013). Such transformation matrices can be obtained from a few thousand aligned words from the source and target side.

Models mentioned above can only work on fixed length text inputs such as words or short phrases, but many tasks in NLP need variable input length. A new extension of these models is Paragraph Vector (Le and Mikolov, 2014) which can convert any variable length input from sentence to document, to a fixed length vector output. Since the Paragraph Vector model training is similar to Word to Vector model, they share many properties and this new model also captures the relationship between similar words and sentences. The previous works on this model show the state of the art results in the field of sentiment analysis and document classification.

As far as we know there has been no previous use of Paragraph Vector model for bilingual and multilingual tasks. Since the Paragraph Vector model is based on Word to Vector model, we get to this conclusion that by using the same method mentioned in (Mikolov et al., 2013) we can build a bilingual Paragraph model to align source and target Documents.

The transformation matrix can be found by solving following optimization problem. In equation (1) x_i is the vector representation of i_{th} source document and z_i is its paired document vector representation in the target space.

$$\min_{W}\left(\sum_{i=1}^{n}\|Wx_i - z_i\|\right) \quad (1)$$

Wcan be found by any optimization method, but we solved it with a stochastic gradient descent approach. By computing $z = Wx$ any source vector will be projected to the target space, then we can search closest neighbors of z in target vectors to find our answers.

Training this model and transformation matrix is relatively fast in comparing with our other modules. Even though this method precision is low, it can discriminate related and unrelated documents from each other very well. Since generating closest neighbors list in this method is simple, this module is used for filtering the target search space for our slower modules such as topic models and machine translation.

3.2 Bilingual Topic Model Module (BiTM)

The basic idea behind topic models is that documents are mixtures of topics, where a topic is a probability distribution over words (Blei et al., 2003). Topic models have a major benefit; they don't need documents to be sentence-aligned, so it will be a good choice for finding comparable corpora. To model bilingual topics, we used an extension of latent Dirichlet allocation (LDA) called Polylingual Topic Model (Mimno et al., 2009). We consider each document as a bag of words, this approach consists of three main steps, first step is creating sets of topics for both sides (source and target languages) then calculating probability of each topic in each document and finally, finding documents similarities.

Figure 2 shows graphical model of polylingual topic model, where α and β are the hyper-parameters on the Dirichlet priors for topic distributions θ and the topic-word distributions φ respectively. This model actually finds and aligns topics of different languages.

Now that the topic distributions of target and source languages are created, we use these topics to find topics probabilities over each document using Gibbs sampling.

Accordingly, each document is converted to a T dimensional vector $v = [p_1, p_2, \ldots, p_T]$, where p_1 is the probability of assigning topic one to this document and T is the number of topics. To find similar documents in two languages we used a well-known method called cosine similarity. In our case, two vectors (from source and target language) are compared, using cosine similarity as bellow:

$$Sim(v',v) = \frac{\sum_{i=1}^{n} v'_i \times v_i}{\sqrt{\sum_{i=1}^{n} (v'_i)^2} \times \sqrt{\sum_{i=1}^{n} (v_i)^2}} \quad (2)$$

Where v' and v are respectively documents of source and target language. The result is a number between 0 and 1, while the similarity of 1, means the documents are completely similar.

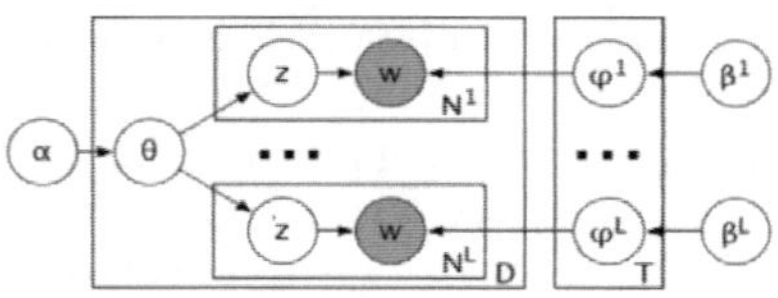

Figure 2. Graphical model of topic model (Mimno et al., 2009)

3.3 Names Module

Named entities play an important role in Cross-Lingual Information Retrieval (CLIR). Comparable documents generally share many named entities (NE) (Gupta and Bandyopadhyay, 2013), in this section, we make a Name model for checking the effectiveness of NEs in aligning comparable documents. In this model, we extract NEs from documents and classify into three types: location, person and organization, then compute document similarity based on the similarity of names that have the same type. As respects NEs usually are phonetically transliterated, we consider the phonetic similarity of the two words as similarity criteria. Our Name model contains two sections:

A. Named Entities Recognition: we apply a CRF-based supervised classifier as NER model.

B. Computing Phonetic Similarity: The main bottleneck in computing phonetic similarity is the lack of availability of transliteration training data so we propose a solution for solving this problem. Our proposed method includes 3 following steps:

3.3.1 Transliteration Mining

In this step, we use an unsupervised transliteration mining model for extracting transliterated names from parallel corpus that is described in (Durrani et al., 2014) and apply this on the Europarl parallel corpus and extract a transliterated bilingual German-English dictionary that we called ENTD (Europarl Transliterated Names Dictionary).

3.3.2 Mapping Table

In this step, we extract high-probability transliterated names of ENTD and apply an iterative alignment model on this for generating a table of characters that are aligned with high probability in source and target languages. This method is similar to the method described in (Mousavi Nejad and Khadivi, 2011). The alignment model is a Levenshtein distance based on the mapping table. In each iteration of the model, the characters with high alignment probabilities added to the mapping table and the algorithm is repeated until no change in the mapping happens anymore.

3.3.3 Compute Phonetic distance

In this step, we compute the phonetic distance between name entities in comparable training documents using a recursive function based on the mapping table. This method is similar to the method described in (Mehdizadeh Seraj et al., 2014). For measuring the distance between an English character in position i and a German character in position j. We will use the recursion definition, according to the following equation. In this definition, e and g are English and German words respectively.

$$d(i,j) = \min \begin{pmatrix} d(i-1,j) + \left(1 - p_{remove(e_i)}\right), \\ d(i,j-1) + \left(1 - p_{remove(g_i)}\right), \\ d(i-1,j-1) + \left(1 - p_{replace(e_i,g_i)}\right) \end{pmatrix} \quad (3)$$

Where p_{remove} and $p_{replace}$ are obtained from the mapping table. Finally, we generate a transliterated bilingual German-English dictionary of transliterated names that have a low phonetic distance, named BTND (BUCC Transliterated Names Dictionary).

3.3.4 Compute Similarity of Documents in Test Time

Computing the phonetic similarity by a recursive function takes a lot of time and it is not efficient for test time, so we use the bilingual dictionaries generated in the previous sections. When there is enough time, we can use the method described in

section 3.3.3 that is a language-independent method. In this state, we divide source-target names in each of the two documents in 3 states: 1. The named entities of the same type that have same letter form. 2. The named entities of the same type that exist in ETND. 3. The named entities of the same type that exist in BTND.
We search each source-target name in state 3 only if it doesn't exist in state 1 and 2, and search it in state 2 only if it doesn't exist in state 1. We also extract URLs from documents and consider these as state 4:

4. The same URLs in two documents.

Finally, we define a score function for computing document similarity between a German document G and an English document E as follow:

$$score_{G,E} = \frac{w_1 s_1 + w_2 s_2 + w_3 s_3 + w_4 s_4}{C_{NE} + C_{url}} \quad (4)$$

Where w_1 is the weight of state 1 and s_1 is the number of common NEs in documents G and E. C_{NE} and C_{url} are the number of NEs and URLs in German documents. For estimating the weight of each state, we apply our models on a development set and increase the impact of phonetic dictionaries ETND and BTND by filtering the pairs of names with low alignment probabilities. We compute the thresholds by testing on the development set.

3.4 SMT Module

When two documents in two different languages are similar, the translation of the first document to the other's language should make a similar document to the second one. That's why we use the statistical machine translation (Brown et al., 1993) as another module for measuring the document similarities.
In this module, we first train a phrase-based SMT system on a sentence-aligned parallel corpus (Zens et al., 2002; Koehn et al., 2003). Then we translate each source document with the trained SMT system, and in the next step, for each source document we calculate similarity scores by comparing its translation to the list of filtered target documents that were produced by the former modules.
For the similarity scores, we use two well-known translation evaluation metrics. The first metric is BLEU, which is computed by comparing the system output against the reference translation (Papineni et al., 2002). Given the precision p_n of n-grams of size up to N (usually N = 4), the length of the translation output in words (c), and the length of the reference translation in words (r), the BLEU metric will be computed as follows,

$$BLEU = BP.\exp(\sum_{n=1}^{4} \log p_n) \quad (5)$$

$$BP = \min(1, e^{1-r/c}) \quad (6)$$

Here the translation output is our SMT system's output for the source document and the reference translation is a target document. As these two documents are not necessarily sentence-aligned we concatenate each of them to make one sentence documents. As we know, one of the BLEU metric's shortcomings is that it was designed for corpus level and might not perform well on single sentences, since the 4-gram precision could be often zero and it makes the whole BLEU score to be zero.
So as BLEU might perform badly in some cases, we also used another metric called Position-independent word Error Rate (PER) (Tillmann et al., 1997). This metric measures a position-independent Levenshtein distance (bag-of-word based distance) between the translation output and reference. The resulting number is then divided by the number of words in the reference.
The reason that we used this instead of other error rates such as WER (Nießen et al., 2000) and TER (Snover et al., 2006) is that it completely neglects word orders. As in our task, sentences in two similar documents might be displaced and we don't want this displacement to influence our similarity score, PER is more reasonable to use.
As the BLEU score contains higher order n-grams, it also considers correct phrases instead of just words in PER, and so it has a higher recall in our experiments (shown in section 4). But as PER might help for the cases that BLUE is not working well, we use both of these scores for our final system.

3.5 System Combination

In our model first the big space of English documents is filtered with high-speed modules. Then for each pair of the documents in this filtered space we compute the value of their features, which is the similarity scores of modules. Scores of TM, Name and SMT modules are used here.

$$(d_i, d_j) \mapsto \left(BiTM(d_i, d_j), Names(d_i, d_j), \mathrm{SMT}(d_i, d_j)\right) \quad (7)$$

Finally, we use a simple linear combination of these features as the final score for the document pairs:

$$Score(d_i,d_j) := W_{TM} \times BiTM(d_i,d_j) + W_{Name} \times Names(d_i,d_j) + W_{SMT} \times SMT(d_i,d_j) \quad (8)$$

In this equation the scores for each pair of documents (d_i,d_j) is used: $BiTM(d_i,d_j)$ is the BiTM score, $Names(d_i,d_j)$ is the Name score, $\mathrm{SMT}(d_i,d_j)$ is two score BLEU and PER of SMT module. The weight of each model is tuned on a development set using Least Square Error approach.

4 Experiments

4.1 Training data

The available data set is a very large corpus of comparable documents, coming from the BUCC shared task. The documents are Wikipedia pages without any links, special tags or Metadata.

Training data (train.en/de) is a corpus of linked comparable documents with about 147(K) documents. The non-linked data are a set of about 166(K) English documents that have no similar document in German document space. Test set (test.en/de) is a random subset of training data that we use its *de* side as the source while ignoring the *en* side. Also, the tuning set for system combination parameters is about 1(K) documents of the training data that are not seen in the test set. Statistical information of data is reported in Table 1.

	#Documents	#Running Words	Lexicon Size
total.en	313471	264(M)	2(M)
train.en	147474	83(M)	1(M)
train.de	147474	121(M)	1(M)
test.en	10000	8(M)	239(K)
test.de	10000	5(M)	263(K)

Table 1. Statistical information of data.

4.2 Preprocessing

The first step of our work is preprocessing the input documents. So that for tokenization and normalization we use the E4SMT tools) Jabbari et al., 2012). This tool normalizes different character representations to be uniform, tokenizes the input text and also tags the specific tokens like numbers, dates, abbreviations, URL addresses, etc. In addition, the compound words of *de* side needed to be split. We have used Cdec tools for this purpose(Dyer, 2009).

4.3 Preparing modules

In this section, we introduce the tools and corpora used for training and preparing each of the modules.

4.3.1 Doc2Vec

Training Doc2Vec module consists of two steps. First we need to train a words vector model. Since the quality of word2vec model depends on the size of the training data, we train our model on all documents in the training and test sets. After this step, we train paragraph vector model and convert each document in source and target test sets to a 200-dimensional vector. After that by selecting 5000 random aligned documents from training set we calculated our transformation matrix by minimizing the error rate on those documents. Training and querying this model for all German documents can be done in several hours. The precision of this module is not very high. Hence, it cannot be used in an effective manner for predicting documents alignment. But due to its speed it can be a great filter for our other modules. The results of this experiment are shown in Figure 4.

4.3.2 BiTM

For training bilingual topic models, we use Mallet toolkit (McCallum, 2002). One important decision in topic modeling is finding the number of topics and the hyper-parameters, because of their significant impact on the resulting topic assignments. For finding the number of topics, we calculate perplexity, which is a way of evaluating the predictive power of the model (Figure 3). From now on, in all the experiments of BiTM we set number of topics to 1200.

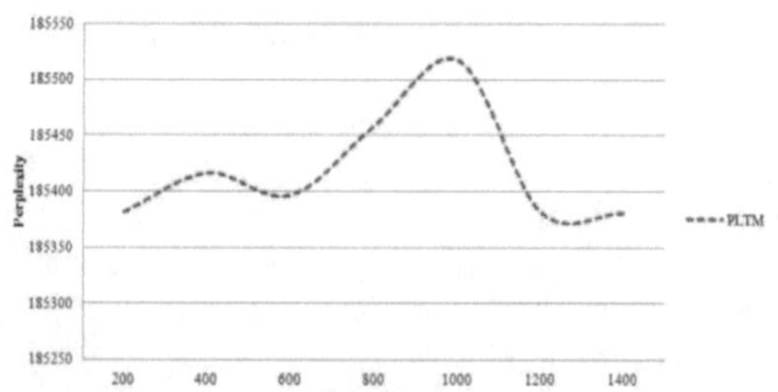

Figure 3. Perplexity for different number of topics. when $\boldsymbol{\alpha} = \mathbf{1}$ and $\boldsymbol{\beta} = \mathbf{0.7}$, the lower perplexity is better.

Also, we use the method in (Wallach, 2009) to find hyper-parameters.

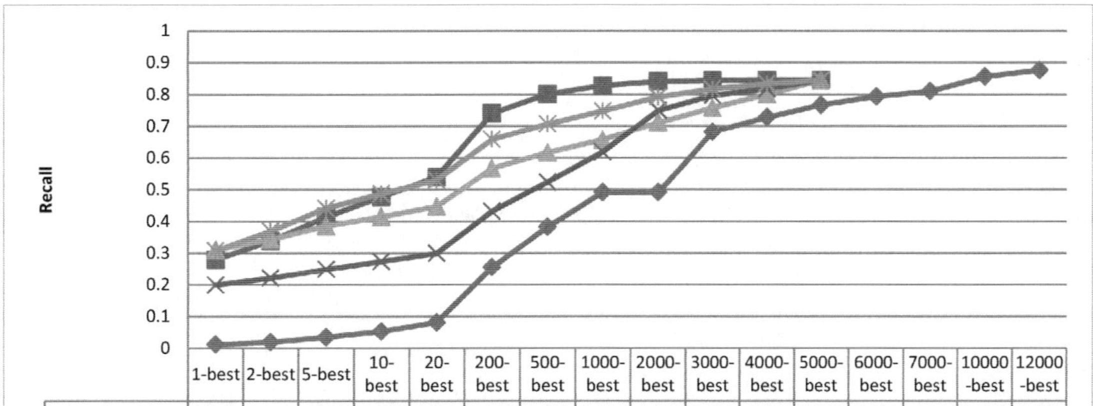

	1-best	2-best	5-best	10-best	20-best	200-best	500-best	1000-best	2000-best	3000-best	4000-best	5000-best	6000-best	7000-best	10000-best	12000-best
Doc2Vec	0.012	0.019	0.035	0.053	0.081	0.255	0.382	0.491	0.491	0.681	0.728	0.766	0.793	0.81	0.856	0.876
TM	0.2789	0.3382	0.4136	0.4773	0.5393	0.7404	0.8002	0.8276	0.8403	0.8437	0.8446	0.8446				
SMT.BLEU	0.3103	0.3433	0.3852	0.4139	0.4465	0.5662	0.6156	0.6564	0.7107	0.7574	0.8001	0.8446				
SMT.PER	0.1986	0.2207	0.2486	0.2736	0.2993	0.4312	0.5229	0.6178	0.7496	0.7963	0.8174	0.8446				
Name	0.3073	0.3696	0.441	0.4868	0.5292	0.6575	0.7062	0.7474	0.7919	0.8167	0.8333	0.8446				

Figure 4. Diagram of modules recall in different neighborhood sizes.

4.3.3 Names

In this work, we use a German and English NER model to tag NEs. For this purpose, we use the Stanford NER tagger tool and also we use an unsupervised transliteration mining with the Moses toolkit[1] (Koehn et al., 2007).

4.3.4 SMT

For this module, we train a German to English SMT system. For this purpose, we use the Moses toolkit for training translation models and decoding, as well as SRILM[2] (Stolcke, 2002) to build the language models. Also, we used the German-English part of the Europarl[3] (Koehn, 2005) parallel corpora as the SMT's training corpora.

4.4 Evaluation

In this phase, we align the documents of test.de set with a proper *en* document from the collection of English documents. In the two filtering steps of the model pipeline, we reduce the size of the target space from 313(K) documents to 5(K) documents for each *de* document. The first filter is the Doc2Vec module, which is the fastest module in our model. This filter reduces the target space to 12(K) English documents that are the nearest documents to the *de* one with 87.6% of accuracy. The second filter is the Name module. This filter reduces the size of the target space from 12(K) documents to 5(K) documents with the accuracy of 84.46%.

Each *de* document in the test set is evaluated with the filtered *en* documents (5K documents). Then the vector of the similarity scores for each pair is produced and the score of the system combination module is computed for each pair of documents. The result is a matrix of similarity values. Finally, for each row of this matrix the 5-best results are extracted.

The precision, recall and F-measure for the 1-best output of the system combination module and the 5-best results list are shown in Table 2.

	5-best results	1-best System Combination
Precision	12.6	45.67
Recall	62.98	45.67
F-measure	21	45.67

Table 2. Results of our model; Precision, Recall and F-measure for 1-best System Combination and 5-best results list.

The final precision of our model is about 12%, this is because of the variation of the modules votes. Each module considers the *en* documents from a different view so the 5-best list of the final results contains the most similar *en* documents to the de input. But from this list just one of them is the exact translation. Although each Wikipedia page has a specific equivalent page in the target language but, it is probable that a set of pages are highly similar to it, especially for pages with related topics. So, because of this characteristic of Wikipedia pages, deciding the exact

[1] https://github.com/moses-smt/mosesdecoder
[2] http://www.speech.sri.com/projects/srilm/
[3] http://www.statmt.org/europarl/

translation just with the content information is a vague task. Also aligning the *de* document to a proper *en* one from a large collection of *en* samples increases this ambiguity.

5 Conclusion

Our work is a framework consists of several modules for retrieving similar Wikipedia pages for German documents from a large collection of English documents. Our model is proper for dealing with very large corpora. The results show that our model is able to find the correct answer in 62% of samples.

The framework proposed here has two advantages over the previous works: firstly it can handle searching through a large collection of data which is achieved by applying the filtering modules. And also everything was done just by using the content information of documents, without using any special tags or Metadata.

Also, all of the modules used in our framework are language independent, and it could be used for any other language pairs.

Acknowledgement

This research was partially supported by targoman.com. We thank our colleagues from targoman.com, who provided insight and expertise that greatly assisted the research.

References

Barrón-Cedeno, Alberto, Paolo Rosso, David Pinto, and Alfons Juan. (2008). On Cross-lingual Plagiarism Analysis using a Statistical Model. In PAN.

Blei, David M., Andrew Y. Ng, and Michael I. Jordan. (2003). Latent dirichlet allocation. the Journal of machine Learning research, 3, 993-1022.

Brown, Peter F., Vincent J. Della Pietra, Stephen A. Della Pietra, and Robert L. Mercer. (1993) .The mathematics of statistical machine translation: Parameter estimation. Computational linguistics 19, no. 2, 263-311.

Manning, Christopher D., Prabhakar Raghavan, and Hinrich Schütze. (2008). An Introduction to information retrieval. Vol. 1. Cambridge: Cambridge university press.

Deerwester, Scott C., Susan T. Dumais, Thomas K. Landauer, George W. Furnas, and Richard A. Harshman. (1990). Indexing by latent semantic analysis. JAsIs 41, no. 6, 391-407.

Delpech, Estelle. (2011). Evaluation of terminologies acquired from comparable corpora: an application perspective. In Proceedings of the 18th International Nordic Conference of Computational Linguistics (NODALIDA 2011), pages 66-73.

Dumais, Susan T., Todd A. Letsche, Michael L. Littman, and Thomas K. Landauer. (1997, March). Automatic cross-language retrieval using latent semantic indexing. In AAAI spring symposium on cross-language text and speech retrieval (Vol. 15, p. 21).

Durrani, Nadir, Hieu Hoang, Philipp Koehn, and Hassan Sajjad. (2014). Integrating an unsupervised transliteration model into statistical machine translation. EACL 2014, 148.

Dyer, Chris. (2009). Using a maximum entropy model to build segmentation lattices for MT. In Proceedings of NAACL HLT 2009, Boulder, Colorado.

Franco-Salvador, Marc, Paolo Rosso, and Roberto Navigli. (2014, April). A knowledge-based representation for cross-language document retrieval and categorization. InProceedings of EACL (pp. 414-423).

Fung, Pascale, and Percy Cheung. (2004). Multi-level bootstrapping for extracting parallel sentences from a quasi-comparable corpus. In Proceedings of the 20th international conference on Computational Linguistics, page 1051. Association for Computational Linguistics.

Gupta, Rajdeep, and Sivaji Bandyopadhyay. (2013). Testing the Effectiveness of Named Entities in Aligning Comparable English-Bengali Document Pair. In Intelligent Interactive Technologies and Multimedia (pp. 102-110). Springer Berlin Heidelberg.

Jabbari, Fattaneh, Somayeh Bakhshaei, Seyed Mohammad Mohammadzadeh Ziabary, and Shahram Khadivi. (2012). Developing an Open-domain English-Farsi Translation System Using AFEC: Amirkabir Bilingual Farsi-English Corpus. In The Fourth Workshop on Computational Approaches to Arabic Script-based Languages (p. 17).

Kilgarriff, Adam. (2001). Comparing corpora. International journal of corpus linguistics, 6, no. 1 (pp. 97-133).

Knoth, Petr, Lukas Zilka, and Zdenek Zdrahal. (2011). Using explicit semantic analysis for cross-lingual link discovery. In Proceedings of the 5th International Joint Conference on Natural Language Processing , pages 2-10.

Koehn, Philipp, Franz Josef Och, and Daniel Marcu. (2003). Statistical phrase-based translation. In Proceedings of the 2003 Conference of the North American Chapter of the Association for Computational Linguistics on Human Language Technology-Volume 1, pp. 48-54.

Koehn, Philipp. (2005). Europarl: A parallel corpus for statistical machine translation. MT summit, (pp. 79-86).

Koehn, Philipp, Hieu Hoang, Alexandra Birch, Chris Callison-Burch, Marcello Federico, Nicola Bertoldi, Brooke Cowan, Wade Shen, Christine Moran, Richard Zens, Chris Dyer, Ondřej Bojar,

Alexandra Constantin, Evan Herbst. (2007). Moses: Open source toolkit for statistical machine translation. Proceedings of the 45th annual meeting of the ACL on interactive poster and demonstration sessions, (pp. 177-180).

Le, Quoc V., and Tomas Mikolov. (2014). Distributed Representations of Sentences and Documents. Int. Conf. Mach. Learn. ICML 2014, vol. 32, pp. 1188–1196.

Li, Bo, and Eric Gaussier. (2010). Improving corpus comparability for bilingual lexicon extraction from comparable corpora. In Proceedings of the 23rd International Conference on Computational Linguistics, pages 644-652. Association for Computational Linguistics.

McCallum, Andrew K.. (2002). MALLET: A Machine Learning for Language Toolkit. http://mallet.cs.umass.edu.

Mcnamee, Paul, and James Mayfield. (2004). Character n-gram tokenization for European language text retrieval. Information retrieval 7, no. 1-2 (pp. 73-97).

Mehdizadeh Seraj, Ramtin, Fattaneh Jabbari, and Shahram Khadivi. (2014). A novel unsupervised method for named-entity identification in resource-poor languages using bilingual corpus. In Telecommunications (IST), 2014 7th International Symposium on (pp. 519-523). IEEE.

Mikolov, Tomas, Ilya Sutskever, Kai Chen, Greg S. Corrado, and Jeff Dean. (2013). Distributed representations of words and phrases and their compositionality. In Advances in Neural Information Processing Systems, pp. 3111-3119.

Mikolov, Tomas, Kai Chen, Greg Corrado, and Jeffrey Dean. (2013). Efficient estimation of word representations in vector space. arXiv preprint arXiv:1301.3781.

Mikolov, Tomas, Quoc V. Le, and Ilya Sutskever. (2013). Exploiting similarities among languages for machine translation." arXiv preprint arXiv:1309.4168.

Mimno, David, Hanna M. Wallach, Jason Naradowsky, David A. Smith, and Andrew McCallum. (2009, August). Polylingual topic models. In Proceedings of the 2009 Conference on Empirical Methods in Natural Language Processing: Volume 2-Volume 2 (pp. 880-889). Association for Computational Linguistics.

Mousavi Nejad, Najmeh, and Shahram Khadivi. (2011). An Unsupervised Alignment Model for Sequence Labeling: Application to Name Transliteration. 2011 Named Entities Workshop.

Navigli, Roberto, and Simone Paolo Ponzetto. (2012). BabelNet: The automatic construction, evaluation and application of a wide-coverage multilingual semantic network.Artificial Intelligence, 193, 217-250.

Nießen, Sonja, Franz Josef Och, Gregor Leusch, and Hermann Ney. (2000). An Evaluation Tool for Machine Translation: Fast Evaluation for MT Research. Proceedings of the 2nd International Conference on Language Resources and Evaluation. Athens, Greece.

Oard, Douglas W. (1998). A comparative study of query and document translation for cross-language information retrieval. Machine Translation and the Information Soup. Springer Berlin Heidelberg, 472-483.

Papineni, Kishore, Salim Roukos, Todd Ward, and Wei-Jing Zhu. (2002). Bleu: a Method for Automatic Evaluation of Machine Translation. In Proceedings of the 40th annual meeting on association for computational linguistics (pp. 311-318). Association for Computational Linguistics.

Potthast, Martin, Benno Stein, and Maik Anderka. (2008). A Wikipedia-based multilingual retrieval model. In Advances in Information Retrieval (pp. 522-530). Springer Berlin Heidelberg.

Smith, Jason R., Chris Quirk, and Kristina Toutanova. (2010). Extracting parallel sentences from comparable corpora using document level alignment. In Human Language Technologies: The 2010 Annual Conference of the North American Chapter of the Association for Computational Linguistics, pages 403-411. Association for Computational Linguistics.

Snover, Matthew, Bonnie Dorr, Richard Schwartz, Linnea Micciulla, and John Makhoul. (2006). A study of translation edit rate with targeted human annotation. Proceedings of association for machine translation in the Americas.

Steyvers, Mark, and Tom Griffiths. (2007). Probabilistic topic models. Handbook of latent semantic analysis 427(7), 424-440.

Stolcke, Andreas. (2002). SRILM-an extensible language modeling toolkit. INTERSPEECH.

Su, Fangzhong, and Bogdan Babych. (2012). Development and Application of a Cross-language Document Comparability Metric. In *LREC*, (pp. 3956-3962).

Tang, Guoyu, Yunqing Xia, Min Zhang, Haizhou Li, and Fang Zheng. (2011). CLGVSM: Adapting Generalized Vector Space Model to Cross-lingual Document Clustering. In IJCNLP , pages 580-588.

Tillmann, Christoph, Stephan Vogel, Hermann Ney, Arkaitz Zubiaga, and Hassan Sawaf. (1997). Accelerated DP based search for statistical translation. Eurospeech.

Wallach, Hanna M., David Minmo, and Andrew McCallum. (2009). Rethinking LDA: Why priors matter.

Winograd, Terry. (1972). Understanding natural language. *Cognitive psychology*, *3*(1), 1-191.

Zens, Richard, Franz Josef Och, and Hermann Ney. (2002). Phrase-based statistical machine translation. In KI 2002, Advances in Artificial Intelligence (pp. 18-32). Springer Berlin Heidelberg.

LINA: Identifying Comparable Documents from Wikipedia

Emmanuel Morin[2] **Amir Hazem**[1] **Elizaveta Loginova-Clouet**[2] **Florian Boudin**[2]

[1] LIUM - EA 4023, Université du Maine, France
amir.hazem@lium.univ-lemans.fr

[2] LINA - UMR CNRS 6241, Université de Nantes, France
{elizaveta.loginova,florian.boudin,emmanuel.morin}@univ-nantes.fr

Abstract

This paper describes the LINA system for the BUCC 2015 shared track. Following (Enright and Kondrak, 2007), our system identify comparable documents by collecting counts of hapax words. We extend this method by filtering out document pairs sharing target documents using pigeonhole reasoning and cross-lingual information.

1 Introduction

Parallel corpora, that is, collections of documents that are mutual translations, are used in many natural language processing applications, particularly for statistical machine translation. Building such resources is however exceedingly expensive, requiring highly skilled annotators or professional translators (Preiss, 2012). Comparable corpora, that are sets of texts in two or more languages without being translations of each other, are often considered as a solution for the lack of parallel corpora, and many techniques have been proposed to extract parallel sentences (Munteanu et al., 2004; Abdul-Rauf and Schwenk, 2009; Smith et al., 2010), or mine word translations (Fung, 1995; Rapp, 1999; Chiao and Zweigenbaum, 2002; Morin et al., 2007; Vulić and Moens, 2012).

Identifying comparable resources in a large amount of multilingual data remains a very challenging task. The purpose of the Building and Using Comparable Corpora (BUCC) 2015 shared task[1] is to provide the first evaluation of existing approaches for identifying comparable resources. More precisely, given a large collection of Wikipedia pages in several languages, the task is to identify the most similar pages across languages.

[1] https://comparable.limsi.fr/bucc2015/

In this paper, we describe the system that we developed for the BUCC 2015 shared track and show that a language agnostic approach can achieve promising results.

2 Proposed Method

The method we propose is based on (Enright and Kondrak, 2007)'s approach to parallel document identification. Documents are treated as bags of words, in which only blank separated strings that are at least four characters long and that appear only once in the document (hapax words) are indexed. Given a document in language A, the document in language B that share the largest number of these words is considered as parallel.

Although very simple, this approach was shown to perform very well in detecting parallel documents in Wikipedia (Patry and Langlais, 2011). The reason for this is that most hapax words are in practice proper nouns or numerical entities, which are often cognates. An example of hapax words extracted from a document is given in Table 1. We purposely keep urls and special characters, as these are useful clues for identifying translated Wikipedia pages.

website major gaston links flutist marcel debost states sources college crunelle conservatoire principal rampal united currently recorded chastain competitions music http://www.oberlin.edu/faculty/mdebost/ under international flutists jean-pierre profile moyse french repertoire amazon lives external *http://www.amazon.com/michel-debost/dp/b000s9zsk0 known teaches conservatory school professor studied kathleen orchestre replaced michel

Table 1: Example of indexed document as bag of hapax words (en-bacde.txt).

Shared Task Paper Proceedings of the Eighth Workshop on Building and Using Comparable Corpora, pages 88–91,
Beijing, China, July 30, 2015. ©2015 Association for Computational Linguistics

Here, we experiment with this approach for detecting near-parallel (comparable) documents. Following (Patry and Langlais, 2011), we first search for the potential source-target document pairs. To do so, we select for each document in the source language, the $N = 20$ documents in the target language that share the largest number of hapax words (hereafter *baseline*).

Scoring each pair of documents independently of other candidate pairs leads to several source documents being paired to a same target document. As indicated in Table 2, the percentage of English articles that are paired with multiple source documents is high (57.3% for French and 60.4% for German). To address this problem, we remove potential multiple source documents by keeping the document pairs with the highest number of shared words (hereafter *pigeonhole*). This strategy greatly reduces the number of multiply assigned source documents from roughly 60% to 10%. This in turn removes needlessly paired documents and greatly improves the effectiveness of the method.

Strategy	**FR→EN**	**DE→EN**
baseline	57.3	60.4
+ pigeonhole	10.7	10.8
+ cross-lingual	3.7	3.4

Table 2: Percentage of English articles that are paired with multiple French or German articles on the training data.

In an attempt to break the remaining score ties between document pairs, we further extend our model to exploit cross-lingual information. When multiple source documents are paired to a given English document with the same score, we use the paired documents in a third language to order them (hereafter *cross-lingual*). Here we make two assumptions that are valid for the BUCC 2015 shared Task: (1) we have access to comparable documents in a third language, and (2) source documents should be paired 1-to-1 with target documents.

An example of two French documents (doc_{fr} 1 and doc_{fr} 2) being paired to the same English document (doc_{en}) is given in Figure 1. We use the German document (doc_{de}) paired with doc_{en} and select the French document that shares the largest number of hapax words, which for this example is doc_{fr} 2. This strategy further reduces the number of multiply assigned source documents from 10% to less than 4%.

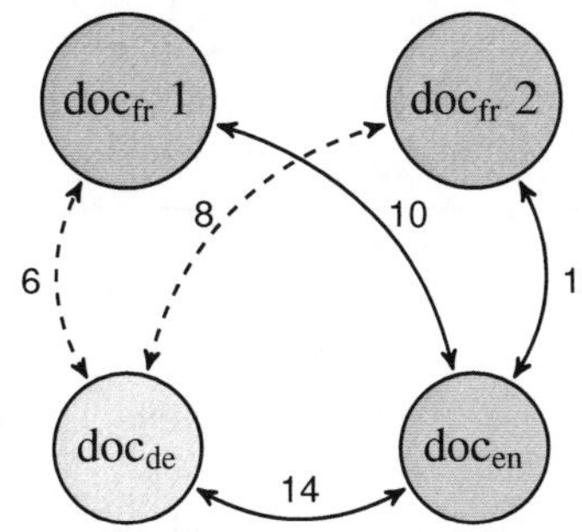

Figure 1: Example of the use of cross-lingual information to order multiple documents that received the same scores. The number of shared words are labelled on the edges.

3 Experiments

3.1 Experimental settings

The BUCC 2015 shared task consists in returning for each Wikipedia page in a source language, up to five ranked suggestions to its linked page in English. Inter-language links, that is, links from a page in one language to an equivalent page in another language, are used to evaluate the effectiveness of the systems. Here, we only focus on the French-English and German-English pairs. Following the task guidelines, we use the following evaluation measures investigate the effectiveness of our method:

- *Mean Average Precision* (MAP). Average of precisions computed at the point of each correctly paired document in the ranked list of paired documents.
- *Success* (Succ.). Precision computed on the first returned paired document.
- *Precision at 5* (P@5). Precision computed on the 5 topmost paired documents.

3.2 Results

Results are presented in Table 3. Overall, we observe that the two strategies that filter out multiply assigned source documents improve the performance of the method. The largest part of the improvement comes from using pigeonhole reasoning. The use of cross-lingual information to

	FR→EN						DE→EN					
	Train			Test			Train			Test		
Strategy	MAP	Succ.	P@5	MAP	Succ.	P@5	MAP	Succ.	P@5	MAP	Succ.	P@5
baseline	31.4	28.0	7.4	32.9	30.0	7.5	28.7	24.9	6.9	29.0	24.9	7.1
+ pigeonhole	57.7	56.4	11.9	–	–	–	61.6	60.1	12.8	–	–	–
+ cross-lingual	58.9	57.7	12.1	59.0	57.7	12.1	62.3	60.9	12.8	62.2	60.7	12.8

Table 3: Performance in terms of MAP, success (Succ.) and precision at 5 (P@5) of our model.

break ties between the remaining multiply assigned source documents only gives a small improvement. We assume that the limited number of potential source-target document pairs we use in our experiments ($N = 20$) is a reason for this.

Interestingly, results are consistent across languages and datasets (test and train). Our best configuration, that is, with pigeonhole and cross-lingual, achieves nearly 60% of success for the first returned pair. Here we show that a simple and straightforward approach that requires no language-specific resources still yields some interesting results.

4 Discussion

In this paper we described the LINA system for the BUCC 2015 shared track. We proposed to extend (Enright and Kondrak, 2007)'s approach to parallel document identification by filtering out document pairs sharing target documents using pigeonhole reasoning and cross-lingual information. Experimental results show that our system identifies comparable documents with a precision of about 60%.

Scoring document pairs using the number of shared hapax words was first intended to be a baseline for comparison purposes. We tried a finer grained scoring approach relying on bilingual dictionaries and information retrieval weighting schemes. For reasonable computation time, we were unable to include low-frequency words in our system. Partial results were very low and we are still in the process of investigating the reasons for this.

Acknowledgments

This work is supported by the French National Research Agency under grant ANR-12-CORD-0020.

References

Sadaf Abdul-Rauf and Holger Schwenk. 2009. On the use of comparable corpora to improve SMT performance. In *Proceedings of the 12th Conference of the European Chapter of the Association for Computational Linguistics*, pages 16–23, Athens, Greece.

Yun-Chuang Chiao and Pierre Zweigenbaum. 2002. Looking for candidate translational equivalents in specialized, comparable corpora. In *Proceedings of the 19th International Conference on Computational Linguistics - Volume 2*, COLING '02, pages 1–5, Stroudsburg, PA, USA. Association for Computational Linguistics.

Jessica Enright and Grzegorz Kondrak. 2007. A fast method for parallel document identification. In *Human Language Technologies 2007: The Conference of the North American Chapter of the Association for Computational Linguistics (NAACL'07)*, pages 29–32, Rochester, New York, USA.

Pascale Fung. 1995. Compiling bilingual lexicon entries from a non-parallel english-chinese corpus. In *Proceedings of the 3rd Annual Workshop on Very Large Corpora (VLC'95)*, pages 173–183, Cambridge, MA, USA.

Emmanuel Morin, Béatrice Daille, Koichi Takeuchi, and Kyo Kageura. 2007. Bilingual terminology mining - using brain, not brawn comparable corpora. In *Proceedings of the 45th Annual Meeting of the Association of Computational Linguistics*, pages 664–671, Prague, Czech Republic, June. Association for Computational Linguistics.

Dragos Stefan Munteanu, Alexander Fraser, and Daniel Marcu. 2004. Improved machine translation performance via parallel sentence extraction from comparable corpora. In Daniel Marcu Susan Dumais and Salim Roukos, editors, *HLT-NAACL 2004: Main Proceedings*, pages 265–272, Boston, Massachusetts, USA, May 2 - May 7. Association for Computational Linguistics.

Alexandre Patry and Philippe Langlais. 2011. Identifying parallel documents from a large bilingual collection of texts: Application to parallel article extraction in wikipedia. In *Proceedings of the 4th Workshop on Building and Using Comparable Corpora (BUCC'11)*, pages 87–95, Portland, Oregon, USA.

Judita Preiss. 2012. Identifying comparable corpora using lda. In *Proceedings of the 2012 Conference of the North American Chapter of the Association for Computational Linguistics: Human Language Technologies*, pages 558–562, Montréal, Canada, June. Association for Computational Linguistics.

Reinhard Rapp. 1999. Automatic Identification of Word Translations from Unrelated English and German Corpora. In *Proceedings of the 37th Annual Meeting of the Association for Computational Linguistics (ACL'99)*, pages 519–526, College Park, MD, USA.

Jason R. Smith, Chris Quirk, and Kristina Toutanova. 2010. Extracting parallel sentences from comparable corpora using document level alignment. In *Human Language Technologies: The 2010 Annual Conference of the North American Chapter of the Association for Computational Linguistics*, pages 403–411, Los Angeles, California, June. Association for Computational Linguistics.

Ivan Vulić and Marie-Francine Moens. 2012. Detecting highly confident word translations from comparable corpora without any prior knowledge. In *Proceedings of the 13th Conference of the European Chapter of the Association for Computational Linguistics*, pages 449–459, Avignon, France, April. Association for Computational Linguistics.

Author Index